INSIGHT ◉ GUIDES

EXPLORE

QUEENSLAND

PLAN & BOOK
YOUR TAILOR-MADE TRIP

BRAZIL **CHILE** **ECUADOR**

TAILOR-MADE TRIPS & UNIQUE EXPERIENCES CREATED BY LOCAL TRAVEL EXPERTS AT INSIGHTGUIDES.COM/HOLIDAYS

Insight Guides has been inspiring travellers with high-quality travel content for over 45 years. As well as our popular guidebooks, we now offer the opportunity to book tailor-made private trips completely personalised to your needs and interests.
By connecting with one of our local experts, you will directly benefit from their expertise and local know-how, helping you create memories that will last a lifetime.

HOW INSIGHTGUIDES.COM/HOLIDAYS WORKS

STEP 1

Pick your dream destination and submit an enquiry, or modify an existing itinerary if you prefer.

STEP 2

Fill in a short form, sharing details of your travel plans and preferences with a local expert.

STEP 3

Your local expert will create your personalised itinerary, which you can amend until you are completely satisfied.

STEP 4

Book securely online. Pack your bags and enjoy your holiday! Your local expert will be available to answer questions during your trip.

BENEFITS OF PLANNING & BOOKING AT INSIGHTGUIDES.COM/HOLIDAYS

PLANNED BY LOCAL EXPERTS
The Insight Guides local experts are hand-picked, based on their experience in the travel industry and their impeccable standards of customer service.

SAVE TIME & MONEY
When a local expert plans your trip, you save time and money when you book, even during high season. You won't be charged for using a credit card either.

TAILOR-MADE TRIPS
Book with Insight Guides, and you will be in complete control of the planning process, from the initial selections to amending your final itinerary.

BOOK & TRAVEL STRESS-FREE
Enjoy stress-free travel when you use the Insight Guides secure online booking platform. All bookings come with a money-back guarantee.

WHAT OTHER TRAVELLERS THINK ABOUT TRIPS BOOKED AT INSIGHTGUIDES.COM/HOLIDAYS

Trip to Portugal

Every step of the planning process and the trip itself was effortless and exceptional. Our special interests, preferences and requests were accommodated resulting in a trip that exceeded our expectations.

Corinne, USA ★★★★★

Trip to Vietnam

The organization was superb, the drivers professional, and accommodation quite comfortable. I was well taken care of! My thanks to your colleagues who helped make my trip to Vietnam such a great experience.

Heather ★★★★★

CONTENTS

ADVENTURE-SEEKERS

4WD the world's largest sand islands – Moreton (route 3), North Stradbroke (route 5) and Fraser (route 8) – catch waves on the Sunshine Coast (route 4) and Gold Coast (route 6), and learn to scuba-dive.

RECOMMENDED ROUTES FOR...

ANIMAL-LOVERS

Hand-feed a wild dolphin at Tangalooma (route 3), snorkel amid kaleidoscopic life on the reef (see page 28) near Cairns (route 10) and the Whitsundays (route 9), and meet a crocodile at Australia Zoo (route 4).

CHILDREN

Whether you're based in Brisbane, with its urban beach and Big Wheel (route 2), or the beach mecca of the Gold Coast (tour 6), it's easy to access the fun-packed theme parks (see page 26).

CULTURE

For music, international exhibitions, or indigenous and modern art, Brisbane (routes 1 and 2) and Cairns (route 10) have galleries and art centres that showcase Queensland's culture.

FOOD AND DRINK

Visit Brisbane's standout bistros (route 1) or Noosa's Hasting Street eateries (route 4) for top-notch food, while Australia's best coffee is grown and brewed on the Atherton Tablelands (route 14).

NATIONAL PARKS

Strap on your walking shoes and hit Queensland's lush national park trails on the Sunshine Coast (route 4), in the Gold Coast hinterland (route 7), Atherton Tablelands (route 14) and en route to Mission Beach (route 15).

NIGHT OWLS

In Brisbane, enjoy a night at the theatre in South Bank's renowned Queensland Performing Arts Centre (route 2) or find a riverside bar (route 1). In Cairns (route 10) visit the casino and the Tanks Art Centre.

ROBINSON CRUSOES

Find peace and solitude on an almost deserted tropical beach in the Whitsunday Islands (route 9). Similar seclusion can be found on the endless empty beaches of North Stradbroke Island (route 5).

INTRODUCTION

An introduction to Queensland's geography, customs and culture, plus illuminating background information on cuisine, history and what to do when you're there.

Brisbane's Story Bridge at night

EXPLORE QUEENSLAND

From the glittering Gold Coast and bustling capital city of Brisbane to the verdant Wet Tropics, where prehistoric rainforest meets the greatest coral reef on earth, Queensland's coastline is an incredible adventure playground.

Size isn't everything, but it is a factor when considering Queensland. This may be only the second-largest state in Australia (after Western Australia), but its 1.73 million sq km (667,000 sq miles) would comfortably swallow several European countries. However, within this vast area there are only around 5 million people – roughly equivalent to the population of Sydney or Barcelona. In cosmopolitan Brisbane and amid the high-rise high-gratification zone of the Gold Coast it can still seem busy, and people-watching is all part of the pull, but travel anywhere else and you'll discover a relaxed, uncrowded and friendly place.

GEOGRAPHY AND LAYOUT

The region covered by the routes featured here is the coast, hinterland and offshore islands between Brisbane and the Gold Coast in the south and Daintree and Cape Tribulation in the north. The routes begin with two walks exploring the historic, entertainment and scenic precincts of the Queensland capital. On Brisbane's doorstep, the natural sand islands of Moreton and North Stradbroke offer scenic 4WD exploration and marine wildlife encounters. Two further easy day trips from Brisbane are provided by the high-rise-backed beaches of the Gold Coast and their counterpoint, the verdant Gold Coast hinterland. The Gold Coast is also the setting for a cluster of theme parks (see page 26).

Heading north, the Sunshine Coast combines an idyllic climate and landscape with gourmet culture, while Fraser Island has a highway of sand for 4WD enthusiasts. In the picturesque Whitsunday Islands, leave your car behind as you island-hop by ferry, camp under the stars and spend your days kayaking and snorkelling.

In Cairns – the capital of far north Queensland and gateway to the Great Barrier Reef – explore the historic town on foot. From Cairns, you can take a ride on a historic train and amazing cable car to and from the market town of Kuranda, or explore the resorts of Port Douglas and Mission Beach, the ancient rainforests of Daintree and Cape Tribulation, and the coffee plantations and waterfalls of the Atherton Tablelands.

Hang-gliding off cliffs near Port Douglas

QUEENSLAND'S HISTORY

About 15 million years ago, the Australian continent broke away from an ancient land mass known as Gondwanaland and gradually drifted northwards to its present location. Due to periodic ice ages, sea levels were lower than today; so low that anyone reaching New Guinea from Asia could continue the journey to north Queensland on foot. These first migrants, ancestors of Australia's Aborigines, arrived some 50,000 years ago.

The first Europeans
It is Dutchman Willem Janssen, who sailed into the Gulf of Carpentaria in 1605, who is generally cited as the first European to 'discover' Australia. Another Dutchman, Abel Tasman, charted parts of Tasmania in 1642 and the northern coast from Cape York to Port Hedland two years later. However, credit for charting the eastern coastline goes to Captain James Cook, whose 1770 voyage opened the way to colonisation.

The penal years
In the late 18th century, the east coast of Australia became a dumping ground for Britain's criminals. In 1788 and 1790, fleets of convict ships arrived at Port Jackson, Sydney's great harbour-to-be, and the colony grew. Cook had noted the presence of fresh water in Moreton Bay back in 1770, while in 1799, Lieutenant Matthew Flinders charted much of the bay but failed to notice the mouth of what is now called the Brisbane River. The river was finally 'discovered' in 1823, when explorer John Oxley was tipped off by some shipwrecked sailors.

An independent Queensland
The first half of the 19th century saw a change in European settlement in Australia. The transportation of convicts was phased out, and by 1860 the continent had been divided into seven colonies, one of which was Queensland. At that time the European population numbered only

Indigenous Queensland

There is no escaping the fact that the indigenous people of Queensland have had a tragic existence since the arrival of European settlers: killed in huge numbers by imported diseases and settlers' guns; living at the mercy of discriminatory laws and damaged by displacement, alcohol and drugs. There have been decades of government funding and more recently there has been official recognition of the mistakes of the past, but many policies have been misguided or mismanaged.

Among Queensland's many notable Indigenous people are the late poet and activist Kath Walker (whose traditional name is Oodgeroo Noonuccal), William Barton, the Brisbane-based Aboriginal didgeridoo player, the artist Judy Watson, and high-profile achievers such as Olympic gold medallist Cathy Freeman and television personality Ernie Dingo.

Tjapukai Aboriginal Cultural Park

23,520, and no industry had yet been established, although gold had been discovered in 1858.

Federation, war and depression

The Commonwealth of Australia, which included the state of Queensland, was born in 1901 and Brisbane was proclaimed a city the following year. When Britain declared war on Germany in August 1914, Australia, as a member of the British Empire, was automatically at war, too.

In 1923, vast silver-lead-zinc deposits were found inland at Mount Isa, but the Depression of the late 1920s and early 1930s was hard on Queensland. In 1934 the Labor Party stimulated the economy through large capital projects, including the construction of Story Bridge and the University of Queensland.

DON'T LEAVE QUEENSLAND WITHOUT...

Meeting a six-foot-tall bird. Your best chance of seeing a cassowary in the wild is around Mission Beach, but don't bank on it – Australia's largest rainforest animal is endangered. See page 82.

Experiencing inland treasures. The coast gets all the press, but be sure to visit the hinterland behind the Gold Coast and Tablelands that overlook Cairns and Port Douglas – these lush hills and plateaus are gorgeous and offer relief from both crowds and oppressive heat. See page 62 and page 90.

Having a close encounter with the Great Barrier Reef. The greatest living organism on the planet is extraordinary up close. Take a snorkel and mask everywhere you go, try an introductory dive, do a day trip or go the whole hog and do a liveaboard dive trip and always make sure you respect its fragility. See page 28.

Riding the ocean waves. Get on a surfboard or paddle across the turquoise waters of the Coral Sea in a kayak or on a SUP board. See page 25.

Loosening your belt. Go on a gastronomic blow out around the fabulous foodie streets of Brisbane – especially James Street, Eagle Street Pier, Little Stanley Street, Merthyr Road in New Farm and Brunswick Street in Fortitude Valley. See page 17.

Going island hopping around the Whitsundays. Seventy-four curvaceous coral cays and tantalising tropical islets lie just begging to be explored by beachcombers, sailors and cast-away types. See page 69.

Earning your off-road wings. Drive a 4WD adventure wagon across the world's biggest sand island, Fraser Island. Watch out for dingoes as you cruise the beach, and keep an eye on the waves for signs of whales. See page 65.

Seeking out an unusual adventure. How about a spot of jungle surfing above the rainforest canopy in the Daintree, or perhaps river snorkelling just outside of Port Douglas? Go with the experts, they know where the crocodiles are... See page 89 and page 84.

Brisbane's General Post Office

Soaking up the sun on the Sunshine Coast

War and boom times

When Britain went to war against Germany in September 1939, Australia once more automatically entered the conflict. Of the 1 million Australian servicemen and women who enlisted, almost 27,000 died.

The 1950s saw the rapid development of the coastal strip south of Brisbane. Originally a secluded holiday destination for Brisbane's middle classes, its property values soared in the post-war period, leading one journalist to dub the area the 'Gold Coast'.

Modern politics: floods and landslides

The long tradition of Queensland being a Labor heartland fell apart in the mid-1950s. After 25 years in power, the party lost the election, ushering in 32 years of rule by the National Party. For two decades until 1987, politics and social life in Queensland were dominated by Sir Joh Bjelke-Petersen, and the era was characterised by confrontation between his government and unions and civil-rights advocates.

When Labor's Peter Beattie – victorious in the 2001 and 2004 elections – retired in 2007, he handed the premiership to Anna Bligh, Queensland's first female premier, who became the first woman to lead her party to a state election victory in 2009.

Between December 2010 and February 2011, large-scale floods devastated Brisbane, killing 35 people and creating a state of emergency. Bligh's handling of the natural disaster was well regarded and she enjoyed a brief period of huge popularity. This was short-lived, however, thanks to vicious infighting within the national Labor party and accusations of the public having been misled over the sale of assets in Queensland. In the 2012 state election, Labor suffered a major defeat and the Liberal party, led by the former Brisbane Lord Mayor, Campbell Newman, was voted in with the biggest majority in the state's history. By 2015, the Labor party had reversed this outcome and Annastacia Palaszczuk was sworn in as Premier of Queensland. Severe weather has caused intermittent flooding with destructive cyclones hitting Queensland in 2015 and 2017.

CLIMATE

Queensland has just two seasons: summer (October–March) and winter. The difference is more pronounced in the south. In the north, there is a wet season (mid-December–April), when rainfall and thunderstorms are common. Northern Australia (which includes Tropical Far North Queensland) endures an annual cyclone season, which officially runs from November to April. Tropical cyclones have made landfall in 2011, 2015, and 2017. The most devastating occurred in 2011, but flooding is common with each.

April to September – the Australian autumn and winter – is often the best time to visit Queensland (particularly the north), as rainfall and temperatures are lower.

Gold Coast high-rises

Brisbane has summer temperatures that range from 20°C to the high 30s (68–86°F plus) and winter temperatures of 10–20°C (35–68°F), with a daily average of eight hours of sunshine. In Cairns the temperature range in winter is 16–26°C (55–90°F) and in summer it can exceed 36°C (125°F), when humidity is also high.

POPULATION AND ECONOMY

According to a 2018 estimate, about 221,000 Aborigines and Torres Strait Islanders live in Queensland, which is 4.4 percent of the total Queensland population. Queensland has one of the fastest-growing populations of any state in Australia. Part of this increase is from overseas migration; Queensland's primary industries – wheat, fruit, cattle, cotton, sugar cane, viticulture, wool and mining – have largely depended on the hard work of immigrants from more than 200 nations. Some have congregated, creating atmospheric and vibrant neighbourhoods, such as South Sea Islanders in Mackay and Italians in Innisfail. However, it is the interstate migrants who are changing Queensland most dramatically. They include a lot of prosperous southern baby-boomers and retirees bringing their wealth north to buy property along the coast.

The influx has coloured the way the rest of Australia views Queenslanders. Historically, the typical Queenslander was defined by the rugged frontier of the far north and outback, with iconic pioneering status as well as conservative values. Another type resides in the southeast corner, a haven for retirees, where poker machines munch through pensions and high-rises shoot up to go one better than their neighbour.

FUTURE CHALLENGES

There are still thousands of kilometres of Queensland coast where anyone can find their own little piece of paradise. Coastal Queensland has boomed on the back of tourism that understandably relies heavily on the state's natural wonders, particularly the Great Barrier Reef, but there are real threats to this idyllic image. Global warming has been implicated in recent coral-bleaching events, mining and agriculture add to harmful sediment flows and, in 2010, a wayward Chinese coal-carrying vessel, the *Shen Neng*, slammed into the Great Barrier Reef, tearing a 1km-long gash into the reef and spewing oil into the Coral Sea, creating a major environmental disaster and highlighting the growing challenges of conserving the beauty in a rapidly developing Queensland. Despite this warning sign, in December 2013 the Australian government gave the go ahead for further mining activity in the region that will see Queensland's Abbot Point coal port dredged to allow access for bigger and increasing numbers of tankers, with the resulting silt to be dumped within the World Heritage-listed area of the Great Barrier Reef. The decision created widespread horror

Bungy-jumping near Cairns

The Glasshouse Mountains

and condemnation from conservation groups, environmental agencies, and the general public within Australia and abroad. In 2015 the government formally banned the disposal of dredge material in the Great Barrier Reef Marine Park alleviating some of these concerns. However, the threats to the Reef continue.

TOP TIPS FOR EXPLORING QUEENSLAND

Sun sense. It's not called the Sunshine State for nothing. Queenslanders have the world's highest rate of skin cancer, but they are learning. Make like a local and slip, slop, slap with the sunscreen (factor 50) and wear hats, sunglasses and – when in the water – rash vests ('rashies').

Get what you pay for. In resorts on the islands, being part of a captive audience can mean paying more for food and drinks. However, if you're not happy with the service you receive in return, tell management about it straight away and give them a chance to make it up to you. Their reputation as a destination depends on happy travellers.

Go bush. Almost all of Queensland's 5-million strong population live around Brisbane or on the coastal strip north to Port Douglas. Tourists mirror this trend, but explore the hinterland and outback areas, where you'll find the most interesting and eccentric people and pubs.

Brisbane on the cheap. Save yourself serious dollars by picking up a Brisbane Five in One Attractions Pack, which gets you into a range of attractions including Lone Pine Koala Sanctuary, Brisbane Ghost and History Tours, Riverlife Adventure Centre, XXXX Brewery Tour and Kookaburra River Cruises.

Be active. Explore as many places as possible on foot, by bike or with a paddle in your hands. Queensland's weather is there to be enjoyed, plenty of places hire bikes, boats and boards, and if you're going to take full advantage of all the great food here, you'll need to burn off those calories somehow.

BYO fun. Take your own snorkelling gear, or buy a good mask, snorkel and set of fins (flippers) as soon as you arrive. Incredible snorkelling opportunities are found around every coastal corner in Queensland and some places (island resorts in particular) charge a huge amount for hourly or daily hire.

Theme park packages. The Gold Coast's major theme parks offer various joint packages that provide discounted entry to two or more parks – shop around to get the best deal.

Be warned. Between the end of November and the middle of December, the Gold Coast, particularly Surfers Paradise, is hit by 'schoolies' – thousands of final-year students on a ritualistic post-exam drunken bender.

Don't become dinner. Saltwater crocodiles live in tidal reaches of rivers, as well as freshwater sections of lagoons, swamps and waterways, and along some beaches and offshore islands. They really are there, and they really might eat you. Always heed warning signs!

Aboriginal bush bread baked over an open fire

FOOD AND DRINK

Queensland's gastronomic credentials are born of two factors: a cultural diversity attracting chefs experienced in some of the world's top cuisines, plus the rich variety of the local produce from tropical seas, rolling pastures and volcanic soils.

Australian cuisine has evolved during 200 years of immigration from almost every country in the world, and the resulting blend of tastes has enriched its dining tables with a huge diversity of cross-cultural concepts. Although British immigrants were in the majority in the early days, Australia's menus were much enhanced by major waves of immigration from China, Italy, Greece and, more recently, Southeast Asia, the Middle East and Africa. In deference to the generally warm subtropical climate, there is now a definite avoidance of some of the heavy, stodgy menus of northern Europe.

The resultant fusion of disparate influences, which tends to disrespect culinary borders, is usually termed modern Australian or 'Mod Oz'. Thus, for example, Asian greens may accompany a Spanish-style seafood dish, the chef relying on the compatibility of the flavours and fresh local ingredients rather than traditional cuisine.

LOCAL CUISINE

The original local cuisine is, of course, 'bush tucker': seasonally available native plants and animals cooked over a camp-fire. The easiest way to sample these flavours in an authentic way is to join an Aboriginal-guided tour or attend an indigenous venue where bush tucker is on the menu. Alternatively, many of Queensland's more experimental chefs are infusing their dishes with native herbs and spices, while kangaroo, emu and crocodile are now commonly found on menus.

A few decades ago, meat and three veg would have summed up a typical Queensland dinner, and a steak was a steak and the bigger the better. Not anymore. Now you must decide between 400-day-old, grass-fed Angus from King Island or 300-day-old Wagyu with 160 days of grain feeding to promote the marbling of the fat. Then there is the decision of which cut to choose and whether to cook it blue, rare or medium. (A quality steak restaurant will never offer to cook a steak 'well done'.)

When it comes to seafood, few places on earth can compete with Queensland. Whatever your taste – be it for molluscs, crustaceans or fish – Queensland has ample varieties and copious quantities sourced from clean waters. When in Brisbane, ask for Moreton Bay bugs: delicious slipper lobsters with excellent sweet

Australian barramundi

white flesh, perfect for Mediterranean and Asian cooking styles. Up north, two species of fish – barramundi and coral trout – vie for top spot in a long list of delicious contenders despite occasional chemical scares. Barramundi ('barra') is an estuarine perch that grows to legendary size and is excellent when cooked bush tucker-style on hot coals, or sizzled on a BBQ plate, or even from a chip shop. Coral trout is a beautiful, spotted tropical reef fish that perfectly suits Asian cuisine.

WHERE TO EAT

Brisbane claims the highest number of restaurants per capita of any city in Australia, and several neighbourhoods and streets have evolved a popular restaurant scene. The cafés and bistros of Eagle Street Pier (www.eaglestreetpier. com.au), James Street (www.jamesst. com.au/food-drink), Park Road in Milton, Brunswick Street in Fortitude Valley, Merthyr Road in New Farm and Little Stanley Street on South Bank, offer good fare in often sophisticated settings. Most Brisbane precincts have a growing selection of ethnic restaurants, the most common being Thai, Indian and Vietnamese. Asian restaurants are mainly concentrated in Fortitude Valley, West End and Sunnybank.

The Gold Coast has more than 5,000 restaurants, ranging from super-casual surf club bistros, such as Northcliffe Surf Club Bistro, to opulent high rise dining rooms. Noosa has a reputation for heavy surf and high quality dining in modish restaurants usually found on or near sophisticated Hastings Street, Noosa Heads.

High-end restaurants

Fine dining is almost exclusively found in the larger commercial centres and upmarket resorts – the sorts of places where you will also find five-star hotels, such as Brisbane, the Gold Coast, Noosa and Cairns, along with the resort islands. And you do not have to look far past the dining rooms of the five-stars to find award-winning chefs performing culinary art for the grateful, and well-heeled, clientele. Brisbane's Cha Cha Char Wine Bar & Grill continues to raise the bar with award-winning wood-fired steaks, and the Gold Coast's Little Truffle delights with five course tasting menus (including a vegetarian one) and Mod Oz cuisine.

Ethnic restaurants

The explosion in inexpensive ethnic cuisine in Australia shows no sign of stopping. Indian, Thai, Turkish, Mexican, Lebanese and Vietnamese have joined the old guard of Italian, Greek and Chinese to rescue folks from resorting to fast food or DIY home cooking, and these are the venues that keep Australia on the cutting edge of the world's cuisine scene. Keep an eye out for the imminent arrival of hipster Asian cuisine (think Peking duck burgers) and even the appearance of a few insects on menus, a la Chinese influence snacks like stir-fried crickets in black bean and chilli. Inland the choice may be

Kangaroo pie in Kuranda

limited to traditional Chinese and pizza, but coastal Queensland, with its cosmopolitan population and massive tourist market, offers a staggering array of ethnic cuisine. Many restaurateurs maximise the cultural experience with careful attention to detail, such as the Ottoman-tent ambience at Ahmets in Brisbane's South Bank.

Pubs and bistros

Again, it is the demands of inbound and international tourism that has boosted coastal Queensland's pubs from mere fuel stops to purveyors of quality food. Along the backpacker trail are barn-sized pubs selling DIY steaks for punters to cook on communal BBQs or hot volcanic rocks – a fun trend whereby the expertise in timing is left to you rather than a professional cook (no room for complaining). Elsewhere, you will find many a gracious old pub that has been gentrified into a restaurant with an attached bar, rather than the other way round, such as the Straddie Pub (officially the Stradbroke Island Beach Hotel) and Port Douglas' s Court House Hotel.

DRINKS

Coffee

Queensland's café scene has exploded over the last few years. Great coffee is grown on the Atherton Tablelands near Cairns, and there are plenty of cafés around that support the local growers and roasters. Expert local coffee roasters including Merlo and Di Bella have helped fuel the boom, as has a move towards alfresco eating, and with the rise of a multitude of hipster-pleasing craft coffee joints around Brisbane, if you shut your eyes (and perhaps get in a cold shower) you could be forgiven for thinking that you're in Melbourne. Sample some seriously good bean juice in Brisbane venues such as Brew, Lady Marmalade, and the Single Guys Coffee Co.

Non-alcoholic drinks

Unsurprisingly, given the tropical climate and the fantastic variety of fruit grown throughout the sunny state, fresh juice bars have become very popular all over Queensland and these are ideal places to get a vitamin and natural sugar fix while attempting to beat the heat.

Wine

The reputation of Australian wines has now fully matured and the country has in excess of 2,500 wineries, many offering cellar-door sales. While the biggest 20 companies produce over 95 percent of Australia's total output, 'boutique wineries' make up well over two-thirds of the total number of wineries. Most people think of the southern states when it comes to wine (oak-driven reds and whites from the Barossa Valley in South Australia and the Margaret River region of Western Australia, Chardonnay and aged Semillons from The Hunter Valley in New South Wales, Cabernet Sauvignon from

Boutique beers   *Bush tucker features fruits of the rainforest*

Coonawarra in the southeast of South Australia, Shiraz from Heathcote in Victoria and Pinot Noir from Tasmania), but Queensland does have an emerging wine industry (www.queensland-wine.com.au). Fabulous fruit wines are produced in the far north, while some award-winning reds and whites have emerged from southeast Queensland, especially in the area called the Granite Belt. Local wines are often light, crisp and fruity, and are designed to complement Queensland's food.

If you're spooked by licensed-restaurant wine prices, it is usually not too hard to find an unlicensed BYO (bring your own wine) restaurant. These restaurants normally charge corkage (per person or per bottle), but it's still much cheaper than buying massively marked-up wine – and there is often a strategically placed liquor outlet nearby.

Beer

Australian beers are famous internationally, and are consumed in vast quantities by their domestic devotees. The most popular brew in Queensland is either Victoria Bitter ('VB') or the local XXXX Bitter (Four X). Queensland's detractors claim that it's called this because few Queenslanders could spell 'beer'. Thankfully, increasing varieties of beer are also becoming available, and brewpubs are flourishing as palates become more adventurous and drinkers less conservative. Boutique breweries have been popping up everywhere from the backstreets of Brisbane to the beach blocks of Burleigh Heads on the Gold Coast, where the excellent Burleigh Brewing Company creates craft beers with names such as Fanny Gertrude's, Black Giraffe and My Wife's Bitter.

Order your Queensland beer in a 'pot' (a 285ml/10oz glass called a 'middy' in NSW or a 'ten' up north) or a schooner (425ml/15oz). In British- or Irish-themed pubs, pints and half-pints normally rule.

Bush tucker

Early European pioneers learnt a lot about 'bush tucker' and bush medicine from the indigenous Aborigines, but their less adventurous countrymen who followed dismissed thousands of years of local knowledge and forced European plants and animals on the land. Two centuries later, many lessons have been learnt, but droughts, weeds and erosion warn that Australians are still learning. Queensland's most celebrated bush food is the macadamia nut, also known as the Queensland nut, which was taken to Hawaii where it became a worldwide commercial success. You will not find many menus dominated by bush foods, but you will find native fruits, vegetables, herbs and spices flavouring many dishes in fine-dining restaurants. In Cairns, try Ochre Restaurant, which utilises indigenous ingredients.

Didgeridoo store at a Kuranda market

SHOPPING

With so much to see and do in Queensland's great outdoors you may be forgiven for leaving the shopping until the last-minute. But the state's department stores, shopping strips, galleries and markets have plenty of bargains.

Throughout Queensland there are ample opportunities to shop for everything from boulder opals to raw cane sugar, didgeridoos to surf gear. Some notable Australian manufacturers have outlets in key shopping and tourism centres – among them is Akubra, whose famous broad-brimmed felt hats have become iconic. To complete the look, check out stockists of RM Williams, the brand named after the late and legendary bushman who designed and sold practical bush-wear to rural Queenslanders for many years. Queensland-produced foodstuffs are now also very popular, including macadamia nuts in various guises, tea and coffee from plantations in Tropical North Queensland, koala-shaped pasta and, for adventurous carnivores, crocodile, shark or emu jerky.

Most shops are generally open Mon–Fri 9am–5pm, with extended evening hours to 9pm on either or both Thursday and Friday. Saturday trading is usually 10am–5pm, while larger stores in big centres or tourist precincts will also trade on Sunday 10am–5pm. The major annual sales are after Christmas (from Boxing Day onwards) and at Easter and mid-year, in the lead-up to the end of the Australian financial year (30 June).

BRISBANE

Brisbane's Queen Street Mall, the centre of the city's shopping scene, offers more than 700 speciality shops spread across two city blocks and 40,000 square metres of retail space, which are dominated by two large department stores, Myers and David Jones, which sell pretty much everything. The attractive, heritage-listed Brisbane Arcade nearby showcases the work of Queensland's award-winning fashion designers.

Fortitude Valley also boasts a number of retail attractions including the TCB Arcade and Licorice Lane. Gail Sorronda, Maryon's, KOOKAÏ, Samantha Ogilvie, and Witchery are just a few of the designer boutiques found on nearby James Street. There is a boutique for everyone.

Some Aboriginal art is unique, and some is mass-produced. The Mitchell Fine Art Gallery, at 86 Arthur Street (www. mitchellfineartgallery.com; Mon to Fri 10am–5.30pm, Sat 10am–5pm) hosts contemporary and aboriginal artists, as well as an annual exhibition.

Sculptures by a local artist at Eumundi Markets

South Bank comes alive with stalls at the weekend for the Collective Markets (www.collectivemarkets.com.au; Fri 5–9pm, Sat 10am–9pm, Sun 9am–4pm), and on a Sunday morning, check out the Riverside at the Gardens (www.theriversidemarkets.com.au; 8am–3pm).

GOLD COAST

The Gold Coast features a number of huge shopping complexes, primary among them the Centro Surfers Paradise. Others are The Oasis shopping centre and Pacific Fair.

The most reputable market on the Gold Coast is Carrara Markets (Sat–Sun 7am–3pm), which is located on the Nerang–Broadbeach Road near Pacific Fair. Aboriginal artefacts are also sold at the new Jellurgal Aboriginal Cultural Centre (1711 Gold Coast Highway, Burleigh; www.jellurgal.com.au; Mon Friday 8am–3pm).

CAIRNS

The main shopping area in Cairns is the Central Business District. There's a lot of variety, from fashion to souvenirs. The Esplanade Markets operate every Saturday (8am–4pm) at Fogarty Park and along the Esplanade. Further out of town, the Tjapukai Aboriginal Gallery (Kamerunga Road, Caravonica; www.tjapukai.com.au), is a showplace of authentic Aboriginal art and artefacts. Kuranda Original Markets (5 Therwine Street; www.kuranda originalrainforestmarket.com.au; daily 9.30am–3pm) make for a great shopping excursion from Cairns.

SUNSHINE COAST

All the produce sold at the thriving Noosa Farmers' Market (Weyba Road, Noosaville; https://noosafarmersmarket.com.au; Sun 6am–noon) is produced by the stallholders. About 15 minutes from Noosa, pretty Eumundi village draws throngs of tourists and locals to its twice-weekly markets (www.eumundi markets.com.au; Wed 8am–1.30pm, Sat 7am–2pm).

Aboriginal art

A piece of Aboriginal art is one of the most emblematic and evocative souvenirs of a visit to Australia. Aboriginal artists sell their work in community art centres, specialist galleries and through agents. Each artist owns the rights to his or her particular stories, motifs and tokens. Dot and bark paintings are the most common forms of Aboriginal art, but look out for contemporary works on canvas, board, boomerangs and didgeridoos, the Aboriginal musical instrument produced in northern Australia from tree branches hollowed out by termites. Boomerangs are always popular; genuine returning and hunting models usually come with instructions to help you throw them properly (and safely).

Bolshoi Ballet dancers at Queensland Performing Arts Centre

ENTERTAINMENT

Queensland's entertainment scene has blossomed visibly over recent years, and concerts, festivals and celebrations now punctuate the events calendar in Brisbane and the Gold Coast, as well as in far North Queensland.

Thanks to a sunny outdoor lifestyle and the popularity of team pursuits, the arts usually play second fiddle to sport. Nonetheless, Queensland has a lot to offer, thanks largely to the changes brought about by World Expo '88 and the development of the Queensland Cultural Precinct in Brisbane's South Bank. Indeed, the Queensland Performing Arts Complex (QPAC; www.qpac.com.au) regularly hosts performers of international renown. Inevitably, the primary cultural focus falls on Brisbane – which has nurtured alternative venues devoted to cutting-edge performances and exhibitions – but with more than 35 percent of the state's population living in regional remote centres, touring has become an essential aspect of taxpayer-funded arts organisations. For more on nightlife, see page 120.

THEATRE

Queensland's acting luminaries include Geoffrey Rush, Diane Cilento, Billie Brown and Deborah Mailman, but new talent spotters should check out Brisbane's stylishly grungy Powerhouse (119 Lamington Street, New Farm; brisbanepowerhouse. org), where primarily avant-garde performances are staged among graffiti and industrial machinery, and the lively Judith Wright Centre of Contemporary Arts (420 Brunswick Street, Fortitude Valley; www. arts.qld.gov.au/judith-wright-centre-brisbane). The delightfully old-fashioned Brisbane Arts Theatre (210 Petrie Terrace; www.artstheatre.com.au) continues to produce drawing-room comedies, mysteries, musical comedies and pantomimes as it has since 1936.

MUSIC AND DANCE

The Sunshine State has produced a plethora of musical talent across a range of genres, and performers and bands that call Queensland home include Savage Garden, Powderfinger, george, Pete Murray, Kate Miller-Heidke, Keith Urban, The Veronicas, The Go Betweens, Tex Perkins and The Saints.

The live music scene in Queensland has continued to evolve over the last few years, with new and improved smaller venues leading the charge. Keep an eye on who is appearing on the bill at intimate places such as the Black Bear Lodge (www.blackbearlodge.com.au; 1/322 Brunswick St, Fortitude Valley) or Brooklyn

Circus performers at the Woodford Folk Festival

Standard (www.brooklynstandard.com.au). In Cairns, the Tanks Art Centre (www.tanksartcentre.com; 46 Collins Avenue, Edge Hill), out by the Botanic Gardens, is an innovative venue featuring assorted musical acts. Brisbane also has a thriving jazz scene, partly centred on the Brisbane Jazz Club at Kangaroo Point, partly in Fortitude Valley bars such as Ric's Bar, The Press Club and The Bowery.

The Queensland Orchestra (www.qso.com.au) delivers a programme of more than 70 concerts annually, while the Queensland Ballet Company (www.queenslandballet.com.au) perform mostly at QPAC's Playhouse – built in 1997 to serve as an ideal venue for theatre and dance – this a must-visit if you are keen on dance.

NIGHTLIFE

The heart of Brisbane's nightlife is Fortitude Valley, aka 'The Valley', which has one of Australia's best live music scenes. For up-to-date gig guides, consult the *Courier Mail*, or for a more extensive list check the online magazine, Scenestr www.scenestr.com.au.

Around the Caxton Street/Petrie Terrace intersection are several good venues: Lefty's Old Time Music Hall (www.leftysoldtimemusichall.com), the Lord Alfred (http://thelordalfred.com.au), a lively pub and restaurant; and The Bowery, 676 Ann Street (www.thebowery.com.au), for a sophisticated locale and cocktails.

Festivals

Brisbane's top festival is the Brisbane Festival (www.brisbanefestival.com.au), featuring a cultural and entertainment smorgasbord staged over three weeks in September. Brisbane Writers Festival (www.bwf.org.au) brings in renowned international authors. The Brisbane Comedy Festival in February–March showcases established and up-and-coming Aussie talent and the annual Festival of Classics, sees hundreds of local classical musicians perform around Brisbane. The Brisbane Pride festival (https://brisbanepride.org.au) celebrates LGBTQ life. The city also hosts a number of others festivals such as St Jerome's Laneway Festival (http://brisbane.lanewayfestival.com), Listen Out (www.listenout.com.au), BIGSOUND Festival (www.bigsound.org.au), or the Music by the Sea Festival (www.musicbythesea.com.au).

Outside Brisbane, events include the two-week Cairns Festival (www.cairns.qld.gov.au/festival) in August, the Festival of the Knob (www.yorkeysknob.com/festival.html) in Yorkey's Knob every Queen's Birthday weekend (June), and the Woodford Folk Festival (www.woodfordfolkfestival.com), held at the end of December. You can also check out the Earth Frequency Festival (www.earthfrequency.com.au) held at Ivory's Rock or the Red Hot Summer Festival (https://sandstonepointhotel.com.au/event/red-hot-summer-2) typically held each March.

Surfing off King's Beach on the Sunshine Coast

ACTIVITIES

Queensland's legendary weather and pristine conditions beckon all visitors to join in the fun, whether it is barracking for a football team, barrelling down a wave or floating around a coral garden surrounded by a swirling rainbow of fish.

Australia is famous for its competitive spirit and robust partisanship when it comes to spectator sports such as football and cricket, but this is a country of doers, not watchers, and this spirit, coupled with the cracking climate and spectacular coastline, combines to form an outdoor mecca. The launch of the Cairns Airport Adventure Festival, which incorporates an Ironman triathlon and numerous running, riding and swimming events open to all, epitomises the participatory approach of the 'Adventurous by Nature' state.

SPECTATOR SPORTS

Four football codes are played in Queensland: rugby league, rugby union, Australian rules and soccer. Rugby League – the most popular – is played at an elite level in the National Rugby League (NRL; www.nrl.com.au) with two Queensland-based teams, the Brisbane Broncos and the North Queensland Cowboys represented. The biggest event in town, however, is when the Queensland Maroons play the New South Wales Blues in the State of Origin series – fiercely parochial matches. Suncorp Stadium (www.suncorpstadium.com.au; Lang Park, Milton, Brisbane)

hosts Queensland's rugby league, rugby union and soccer matches. The Brisbane Cricket Club more commonly known as the Gabba (https://thegabba.com.au; Vulture Street, Woolloongabba, Brisbane) is the home ground of the Brisbane Lions, Queensland's only AFL (Australian Football League) team, and it also hosts major cricket matches (including the all-important Queensland Ashes test).

OUTDOOR ACTIVITIES

Bushwalking

The Queensland government has progressively established walking tracks through some of the most beautiful parts of the state as part of its 'Great Walks' programme. More information about these walks and many others is available from the Queensland Walks website (www.queenslandwalks.org.au) and the Department of National Parks, Recreation, Sport and Racing (www.nprsr.qld.gov.au).

Golf

Queensland has built a reputation for its golf-resort courses, with more than 10 on the Gold Coast and others on the Sunshine Coast and further north near

On the beach at Port Douglas

Sea kayaking near Cairns

the Whitsundays and Port Douglas. Golf Queensland (www.golf.org.au/queensland) provides information on public-access courses.

Sailing

Boating enthusiasts are drawn to the 74 islands of the Whitsundays, where even novices are permitted to go 'bareboating' (cruising the calm waters without any crew). Dozens of operators hire yachts and catamarans at Airlie Beach and Shute Harbour. To begin arranging boat charter, see the Whitsunday Tourism website (www.tourismwhitsundays.com.au) or contact the Whitsunday Central Reservation Centre (tel: 4946 5299).

Sea kayaking and SUPing

Sea kayaking is popular all over the state, and hundreds of operators offer kayak hire and guided paddling tours. See page 72 for one example of a kayaking tour in the Whitsundays. SUP (stand-up paddle boarding) is a relatively sport that is enormously popular in Queensland's ideal conditions; it's possible to hire boards in many places.

Surfing

Queensland's surf beaches are concentrated in the southern corner of the state, where there's no reef to interrupt the swell. Surf schools include Cheyne Horan's School of Surf (Surfers Paradise; www.cheynehoran.com.au) and Godfathers of the Ocean (Surfers Paradise; www.godfathersoftheocean.com).

Cycling

Humidity and heat aside, cycling in Queensland is fantastic. Cairns, which held the Mountain Biking World Championships in 1996, was right at the front of mountain biking as it evolved as a sport, and Smithfield is a mecca for fat-tyre fans. Cairns is hosted several recent MTB World Cup events including the return of the World Championships in 2017. You can hire bikes and ride these trails and a multitude of others around the state. Road riding is popular too. Bicycle Queensland (www.bq.org.au) has information on bicycle-user groups, cycle paths and ride programmes, and the Transport Queensland website (www.transport.qld.gov.au/cycling) also carries information on cycle routes and maps published by local councils from the Gold Coast to Townsville.

Snorkelling and diving

Seeing the Great Barrier Reef up close is a must-do for any visitor to Queensland. Water temperatures stay warm all year round, but August through to January generally offers the best visibility. Scuba-diving in Queensland is highly organised, and a large number of reputable operators offer quality training courses (see page 29). Snorkelling, however, can be just as much fun, with no time limit and almost no cost. Buy or bring your own mask, snorkel and fins, as some places charge a fortune for hire. Always respect the reef – don't take 'souvenirs'!

Thrills on a Dreamworld rollercoaster

GOLD COAST THEME PARKS

For adrenalin junkies, energetic teens and big kids, the over-the-top theme parks of the Gold Coast provide more than enough exhilaration, thrills and action to occupy a day or three.

Whatever your hobby or obsession, the Gold Coast probably offers it in the form of a 'world' or a theme park. There's Wet 'n' Wild Water World, Dreamworld, Iceworld, Sea World, Snooker World, Tropical Fruit World, Warner Brothers Movie World, and Whitewater World just to mention a few, all dishing up folly, fun, fear, fact, fantasy and fast food.

The ethics of keeping animals in captivity is an issue that is fraught with controversy, as illustrated by the release of *Blackfish* in 2013, a documentary which highlighted the horrendous plight of the orcas at Sea-World Orlando (unaffiliated with Sea World Gold Coast). Although Queensland's Sea World does not keep orcas and claims to promote conservation through the rehabilitation of sick, injured or orphaned wildlife, it does have dolphins, sharks and polar bears in captivity. In recent years there have been several demonstrations by animal rights campaigners to end the practice of 'animals for entertainment', directed not only at Sea World but also Dreamworld, which has a tiger attraction.

SEA WORLD

Sea World (Seaworld Drive, Main Beach; www.seaworld.myfun.com.au; daily 9.30am–5pm) on the Southport Spit has developed its rides and performances in parallel with a programme of marine animal rescue and welfare, but we do not recommend visiting, and thus supporting, events with performing animals.

Shark Bay comprises two main lagoons inhabited by various species of sharks. It is possible for visitors to scuba-dive and snorkel amongst the sharks and touch (very carefully) some of the smaller sea creatures. Another attraction is the **Meet the Dolphin show**, in which the trained dolphins join equally well-rehearsed humans in the world's largest naturalistic lagoon habitat.

More unusually, Sea World also has a polar attraction – **Polar Bear Shores** – in an as-near-to-natural-as-possible Arctic summer environment, created with the use of wind generation, misting and fogging, and rain simulation, as well as natural vegetation.

Hollywood Stunt Driver show at Warner Brothers Movie World

DREAMWORLD AND WHITEWATER WORLD

Ever wondered what it feels like to fall backwards off a 38-storey building? **Dreamworld** (Dreamworld Parkway, Coomera; www.dreamworld.com.au; daily 10am–5pm, extended hours during school holidays) provides a pretty good simulation of exactly what that experience would feel like with the **Tower of Terror II** ride, the world's fourth tallest roller coaster. The park also offers a sliding scale of less alarming diversions, ranging from the Claw and the Wipeout to rides on rollercoasters, chairlifts, paddle steamers and trains. There is also an IMAX adventure theatre and native (and some international) wildlife, including dingoes, kangaroos, koalas, and Tiger Island.

Next door, and under the same management, is **Whitewater World** (Dreamworld Parkway, Coomera; www.whitewaterworld.com.au; daily 10am–5pm). Terror, temporary weightlessness, whitewater, plunging, whirlpools and general carnage – that's what you pay your money for here, and that's just during one ride: The Rip. After that you can check out the massive funnel, the Green Room, and various slides, wave pools and tubes, all of which ensure you get drenched (one, rather worryingly, is called 'The Wedgie').

WARNER BROTHERS MOVIE WORLD

Warner Brothers Movie World (Pacific Motorway, Oxenford; www.movieworld.com.au; daily 9.30am–5pm) invites you to enjoy a well-presented, behind-the-scenes view of the illusions involved in movie making. One of its most popular attractions is **Hollywood Stunt Driver 2**, a simulation of an action movie set with plenty of thrills and spills – all in the best Hollywood tradition. Newer to the line-up is a 3D alien shoot-em-up interactive game called Justice League. It joins a family favourite, the Lego Movie 4-D Experience, with spectacular special effects, and some hair-raising rides, such as the **Batwing Spaceshot**, the **Doomsday Destroyer**, and the **Superman Escape** rollercoaster, where riders are hurled upwards at a speed of 100kph (60mph) and accelerate from 0–100kph in two seconds.

WET 'N' WILD WATER WORLD

Young kids and older thrill-seekers are well catered for at **Wet 'n' Wild Water World** (Pacific Motorway, Oxenford; www.wetnwild.com.au; daily 10am–5pm, later in summer). Young children can head to **Wet 'n' Wild Junior**, while older adrenalin junkies will love **Extreme H2O Zone** with its huge slides and high-speed rides, including the Black Hole – a tube slide that sends you spiralling through utter darkness. Other highlights are the **Giant Wave Pool** and a 15-minute tube ride along a slow-moving river from the simulated tropical island's **Calypso Beach**.

Learning to dive

GREAT BARRIER REEF

The Great Barrier Reef, a protected Unesco World Heritage Site, is one of the most beautiful and diverse natural phenomena and the largest living organism in the world. Its full wonder and glory are accessible to anyone who can don a mask and snorkel.

The Great Barrier Reef, one of the Seven Natural Wonders of the World, is an aquatic wilderness bigger than the UK, Holland and Switzerland put together. The reef extends over 250,000 sq km (96,500 sq miles) and comprises some 3,000 individual coral reefs and 940 islands running along the Queensland coast from north of Cape York Peninsula to just north of Fraser Island.

Declared a World Heritage Site in 1981, it is an extraordinarily complex ecosystem, a dazzlingly beautiful universe of low-wooded islands, mangrove estuaries, sea-grass beds, algae and sponge gardens, sandy and coral cays, mud floors and deep ocean troughs.

The largest structure built by living organisms on earth, the reef contains one-third of the known species of soft corals and more than 400 hard corals. It is also the home of 1,500 species of fish, dugongs, marine turtles, dolphins, whales, sea snakes, birds, and sharks.

WHEN TO SEE THE REEF

The weather will play an important part in your experience of the reef. From late April through to October it is at its best,

the clear skies and moderate breezes offering perfect conditions for coral-viewing, snorkelling, diving and swimming. In November the first signs of the approaching 'wet' appear: variable winds, increasing cloud and showers. By January it rains at least once most days.

Even in winter the water is never cold, but it's worth paying a couple of dollars extra to hire a wetsuit anyway; most people find it hard not to go on snorkelling for hours in this extraordinary environment.

October to May is stinger (jellyfish) season in North Queensland. Although not considered a great risk when swimming on the outer reefs, stingers are potentially deadly, and stinger suits can act as a preventative measure and also offer great protection from the sun. Stinger suits should be offered to guests on diving and snorkelling trips, sometimes for hire, sometimes for free.

HOW TO SEE THE REEF

One of the easiest ways to visit the reef is to take a day trip from Cairns, Port Douglas, Airlie Beach or Cape Tribulation. Almost all day trips follow a similar format: a morning dive, followed by a buffet lunch,

Exploring Osprey Reef   *Reef sharks*

then, assuming you've not eaten too much or partaken of free beer, an afternoon dive. There should be a marine biologist on board, who will explain the reef's ecology. Before you book, also ask about the number of passengers the boat takes; this varies from several hundred to fewer than a dozen on smaller craft.

Learn to dive

While snorkelling the reef satisfies many, you might want to learn to dive to maximise your experience. Recommended dive schools in Queensland include: Deep Sea Divers Den (www.diversden.com.au); Prodive Cairns (www.prodivecairns.com), Blue Dive Port Douglas (http://bluedive.com.au), and Tusa Dive (www.tusadive.com). These provide dive courses as well as organised dive trips (see page 25). For more, visit www.padi.com.

Day-trip operators

By no means a comprehensive list, the following operators run day trips to the reef. **Great Adventures** (Reef Fleet Terminal, 1 Spence Street, Cairns; www.greatadventures.com.au) runs several options to Green Island, only 45 minutes from Cairns, as well as to a pontoon on the outer reef with semi-submersibles and underwater observatory. Also in Cairns, **Reef Magic** (Reef Fleet Terminal, 1 Spence Street; www.reefmagic.com.au) offers the chance to spend five hours at their Marine World pontoon at Moore Reef, with semi-submersible, optional

guided snorkelling tours and helicopter flights. **Cruise Whitsundays** (www.cruisewhitsundays.com), operating out of Hamilton Island, offers day trips as well as a special overnight package which provides an opportunity to spend two days at the reef and a night on the water, under the stars.

The wave-piercing catamarans of **Quicksilver Cruises** (Marina Mirage; www.quicksilvergroup.com.au/quicksilver-cruises.html) based in Port Douglas, speed out to a floating platform at Agincourt Reef with an underwater observatory and semi-submersible vessel.

Cruises and live-aboard vessels

Live-aboard vessels provide fully catered voyages where you overnight at sea to maximise the time spent on the reef. Voyages usually range from three to seven days, and the price includes all meals, entertainment and activities. Usually, but not exclusively, catering to experienced divers, live-aboard trips offer dive instructors and/or marine biologists along with the benefits of small-group touring. One of the most experienced and best operators is **Mike Ball Dive Expeditions** (www.mikeball.com; 3 Abbott Street, Cairns), which runs three- to 10-day cruises departing from Cairns.

Great Barrier Reef islands

Numerous continental islands and coral cays within the Great Barrier Reef region offer resort accommodation,

Deep–sea divers

from camping to luxury. The following is a small selection:

Green Island (www.greenislandresort. com.au). A coral cay with an eco-sensitive resort. A popular day-trip destination from Cairns.

Hamilton Island (www.hamiltonisland. com.au). The major resort island in the Whitsunday group, accessed from Airlie Beach, with numerous accommodation and tour options.

Heron Island (www.heronisland.com). Accessed via Gladstone, a coral cay with one boutique resort and miles of coral reef.

Fitzroy Island (www.fitzroyisland.com) A short hop from Cairns, with a newly reopened resort, lots of good snorkelling, a turtle hospital and a PADI dive centre.

Lizard Island (www.lizardisland.com. au). A remote continental island, accessed by air from Cairns, with access to the famous Cod Hole and Osprey Reef dive sites, and a five-star resort.

Magnetic Island (www.magneticisland.com.au). A delightfully unpretentious island, accessed by sea from Townsville, with several budget and mid-range accommodation and tour options.

Orpheus Island (www.orpheusisland. com). Out-of-the-way Orpheus is a luxurious retreat with just 14 luxury, secluded rooms, suites, and villas. Access is via a 30 minute helicopter ride from Townsville or 90 minutes from Cairns.

EXPERIENCING THE REEF

Every morning, dozens of state-of-the-art dive boats and wave-piercing catamarans head out from Cairns and Port Douglas to the outer reef. About an hour later, regardless of their departure point, they will be moored over the coral. Because the water is so shallow, snorkelling is a perfectly satisfactory way of experiencing the brilliant colours of the reef and marine life. Many people prefer it to the more technical scuba-diving; even so, most boats offer tanks for experienced divers and 'resort dives' for people who have never dived before.

As soon as you poke your head underwater, the world erupts. It's almost sensory overload: there are vast forests of staghorn coral, whose tips glow purple like electric Christmas-tree lights; brilliant-blue clumps of mushroom coral; layers of pink plate coral; and bulbous green brain coral. Tropical fish slip about, showing off their fluorescent patterns: painted flutemouth, long-finned batfish, crimson squirrel fish and hump-headed Maori wrasse. You should not interfere with any of the life on the reef, which is why buoyancy control is so important, and definitely do not touch a poisonous barbed stonefish.

The course of Australian history might have been very different had Commander James Cook been less fortunate when his ship *The Endeavour* ran aground on the reef in June 1770. Thirty shipwrecks lie in the reef's waters and experienced divers will enjoy exploring them.

Snorkellers by their dive boat

Green Island is easy to reach from Cairns

Flying is an alternative way to experience the reef, and from the air you can often spot migrating whales and sea turtles. **Check the Cairns Visitor Centre** website (www.cairnsvisitorcentre.com) for their featured providers who generally offer several tours combining a landing at Green Island and the chance to snorkel the reef.

THREATS TO THE REEF

In December 2013, the Australian government controversially gave the go ahead for increased industrial activity around the Great Barrier Reef – a decision that paved the way for dredging, dumping and increased shipping traffic within the protected area. The decision – taken only a few years after a Chinese tanker ran aground on the reef, tearing a huge gash in the coral and haemorrhaging thousands of litres of oil into the fragile eco system – drew widespread horror and condemnation from conservation groups, environmental agencies and the general public in Australia and abroad, and has led to concerns that Unesco will label the Great Barrier Reef as endangered. In January 2019, the Marine Park Authority granted approval for North Queensland Bulk Ports to continue to dump maintenance dredge spoil within the park's boundaries. This came just days after extensive flooding in Queensland spilled large amounts of sediment into the park. It is clear that the protection and conservation of this fragile site remains at risk.

Other major threats to the health of the reef include coral bleaching. If the clear, tropical waters remain too warm for too long, corals expel their photosynthesising zooxanthellae and become colourless. Bleached corals are not necessarily dead and can regain their original algae if not too stressed, but if the water doesn't cool within about a month the coral will die. Up to five percent of the Great Barrier Reef has been severely damaged during each of the last two major bleaching events, with increased temperatures as a result of climate change being the most obvious culprit.

Corals are also damaged by boat anchors, sewage from resorts, and by divers and snorkellers. The dugong and all six of the reef's marine turtle species are threatened because of the loss and degradation of their habitat.

Coastal wetland forest is still being cut down to make room for the beef cattle, sugar cane, cotton industries and banana plantations close to the coast and hundreds of reefs are at risk from the sediment and chemical run-off from farming, and from the loss of the coastal wetlands that have acted as a natural filter in the past.

About a fifth of Queensland's population lives along the coast adjacent to the reef, and with the current interstate and overseas migration to the state (over 200 people each day), communities continue to grow. How to manage water quality, tourism and commercial and recreational fishing is a major concern.

Tugging a cargo ship in Brisbane Harbour, 1891

HISTORY: KEY DATES

Aborigines lived in Queensland for 50,000 years before the arrival of Captain Cook. An energetic population – explorers, emancipated convicts and settlers – later carved out a life here. Today, the Gold Coast is the nation's fastest-growing region.

BEFORE THE EUROPEANS

c.50,000 BC   The first humans arrive in Australia from eastern Asia, via New Guinea, travelling on foot.

THE FIRST EUROPEANS

1770   On 22 August Captain James Cook, aboard the *Endeavour*, raises the Union flag on Possession Island, Cape York, and claims eastern Australia for King George III.

1799   Explorer Matthew Flinders names Redcliffe Point, which becomes the site of Queensland's first European settlement.

1824   First convicts and jailers arrive at Redcliffe, on Moreton Bay.

1831   Convict population peaks at 947.

1842   Brisbane is declared open for free settlement.

1846   Schooner *Coolangatta* wrecked. Brisbane becomes a port of entry.

1848   Queensland's first immigrant ship, *Artemisia*, reaches Moreton Bay.

STATEHOOD

1859   Statehood comes with separation from NSW and the naming of Queensland (European population 23,520).

1860s   Sugar planted at Redland Bay, providing a ready source of rum.

1887   Brisbane connected by rail to Sydney. Difficulties (which still exist) arise because of Queensland's choice of narrow gauge, which did not match that of the southern states.

1901   On 1 January Australia's six independent colonies are federated into the Commonwealth of Australia.

WAR AND BOOMTIME

1914   Australian troops join the allies in World War I.

The procession of the 41st Battalion through Brisbane on Anzac Day, 1916

1915   On 25 April, ANZAC troops begin the Gallipoli campaign in Turkey, which results in major loss of life.

1933   Surfers Paradise township is named after hotelier James Cavill's hotel of the same name.

1939   Outbreak of World War II: Australian forces fight in Europe and the Middle East. Later in the war, Australia's military forces fight the Japanese in the Pacific theatre.

1941   First convoy of US servicemen arrives in Brisbane, which becomes a large military base.

1959   The city of Gold Coast is established.

1974   Cyclone Wanda crosses the coast. Brisbane's worst flood since 1893.

1982   The 12th Commonwealth Games held in Brisbane.

1988   Australia celebrates its bicentenary. Brisbane hosts World Expo '88.

1992   Australian High Court rejects *Terra Nullus* (empty land) concept; theoretically great swathes of Crown Land could be claimed by Aboriginal groups under Native Title law.

21ST CENTURY

From 2000   Fed by immigration from the south, Queensland's population grows at twice the national rate.

2005   Brisbane launches its long-range bid for the 2024 Olympics.

2007   Brisbane's Gallery of Modern Art (GoMa) opens its doors.

2011   In January the Brisbane area floods, killing 38 people, and three quarters of the state of Queensland is declared a disaster zone. In February, Severe Tropical Cyclone Yasi leaves a trail of carnage across northern Queensland.

2011   Cairns Adventure Festival launched, incorporating an Ironman triathlon and numerous other events.

2013–14   Australian government approves increased shipping and industrial activity within Great Barrier Reef Marine Park, sparking environmental concerns about the future of the reef.

2015   The Australian government formally bans the disposal of capital dredge material in the Great Barrier Reef Marine Park

2016   The Redcliffe Peninsula railway line opened to passengers a 'mere' 131 years after it was initially proposed

2017   Tropical Cyclone Debbie made landfall causing severe power outages and flash flooding. Some 23,000 are forced to evacuate.

2018   The Commonwealth Games are held on the Gold Coast, the 5th time Australia hosted.

2019   The Australian government authorises the dumping of dredge spoil into the GBR Marine Park.

2020   The Australian PGA Championship takes place in Queensland.

BEST ROUTES

Story Bridge

BRISBANE CITY CENTRE

This stroll around Brisbane's Central Business District (CBD) unveils Queensland's colonial history, showcases architectural landmarks and taps into the bustle of one of Australia's fastest growing cities. On the way, discover its wild and natural corners, shopping bazaars and dining scene.

DISTANCE: 6km (3.75 miles)
TIME: A half-day
START: Riverside Centre
END: Brisbane Arcade
POINTS TO NOTE: Let the weather influence your pace and timing on this walking route and remember your sunscreen, hat and water. Along the way there are numerous places to buy a drink and catch some breeze in the shade by the river. Although there is one hill, the steep climb comes early on in the tour, and overall it is not a particularly strenuous walk.

As it meanders towards the coast, Queensland's longest river, the Brisbane, makes a deep loop around Spring Hill, the location of Brisbane's CBD and the heart of the city. This part of town lies about 20km (12 miles) upstream from where the river empties into Moreton Bay.

An excellent introduction to Brisbane is the City Sights bus tour (www.citysights.com.au). Buses leave every 45 minutes from 19 stops, with the first bus leaving Post Office Square at 9am and the last bus departing from there at 3.45pm. There's informative commentary, and you can hop off and hop on a following bus to explore at your own pace. Your ticket permits same-day travel on CityCat ferry services.

Historical development

To the indigenous Yuggera people, this mangrove-lined bend in the river was a traditional fishing ground and the location of a crossing point known as Min-an-jin.

The Moreton Bay penal settlement – the last major port to be established in the colony of what was then New South Wales – was founded in 1824 for the resettlement of repeat offenders from Sydney. Initially located at Redcliffe, in in 1825 the settlement was moved to North Quay, the site of the present-day CBD to improve security and gain access to a reliable supply of fresh water: the spring-fed creeks running off Spring Hill. In 1842 Britain closed the Moreton Bay penal settlement and declared the area open to free settlers. Private enterprise soon grasped the opportunities for

Customs House   *Commissariat Store*

growth, and the settlement's population grew to almost 6,000 by the time Queensland became a self-governing colony in 1859, with Brisbane anointed as its capital.

Today's bustling city barely has time to acknowledge its past, as new skyscrapers continue to vie for the title of Brisbane's tallest. Perhaps a late developer compared to its southern siblings, Brisbane is now making up for lost time and shows no sign of slowing down or looking backBrisbane River

Start from the architecturally acclaimed highrise **Riverside Centre** and **Riparian Plaza**, which dominate the Riverside Precinct. Have breakfast at the **Aquila Caffe Bar,** see ❶, and watch the City-Cat ferries beetle under Story Bridge (see page 40) to disgorge well-dressed commuters at the pier. Also look out for climbers on the top girders of Story Bridge – if you feel like joining them, check out Story Bridge Adventure Climb (www.sbac.net.au).

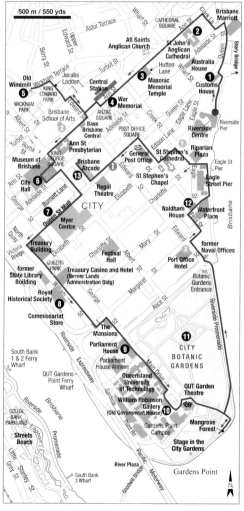

The Old Windmill

CUSTOMS HOUSE

Head north (downstream) along the Riverside Promenade and after a few hundred metres the stately, copper-domed **Customs House** ❶ comes into view. This colonnaded example of Victorian architecture was constructed in 1886–9; it is now owned by the University of Queensland and provides an interesting visual contrast to the glass skyscrapers towering behind. Climb the well-worn sandstone stairs to emerge on Queen Street. The impressive 1888 facade opposite is what remains of a warehouse, indicating, along with the Customs House itself, the significance of river trade during the boom-time of the late 1800s.

Turn right and walk along Queen Street to the intersection with Adelaide Street. Cross here and ascend the narrow Clark Lane to Ann Street and turn left.

ST JOHN'S CATHEDRAL

Ann Street boasts several significant religious buildings, but taking pride of place is the Gothic Revival **St John's Anglican Cathedral** ❷ with its soaring steeple at No. 373. The foundation stone was laid in 1901, but construction continued on and off for over 100 years. Architecture buffs will be excited by Australia's only example of a vaulted ceiling constructed entirely of stone.

Continue southwest down Ann Street. Just past Hutton Lane on the left is the impressive facade of the **Masonic Memorial Temple** ❸ (No. 311; tour hours vary; free) with its four-storey-high columns. Built in 1930, the temple has a striking Grand Hall and Grand Foyer.

ANZAC SQUARE

Keep walking downhill along Ann Street and cross Creek Street. The clock tower of **Central Station** is soon on your right, and directly opposite is the poignant **ANZAC Square War Memorial and Parkland** ❹. The **Shrine of Remembrance** features an eternal flame and 18 columns representing 1918, the year that peace was declared after World War I. Beneath is an underpass to Central Station and a **World War II Shrine of Memories**.

Cross over Ann Street to Central Station, and continue towards the Edward Street intersection. On the corner diagonally opposite is the elaborate Base Brisbane Central hostel building, which was built for the Salvation Army in 1911.

KING EDWARD PARK

Turn right at Edward Street, and climb the hill to cross over Turbot Street and enter **King Edward Park**. The entrance to the park is guarded by three striking bronze sculptures looking like props from a sci-fi movie. Panels reveal they are actually sets from a classical play, *Agamemnon*. Behind the sculptures, the bright red steps of **Jacobs Ladder** lead you towards **Spring Hill** and the

Detail on Brisbane City Hall

Anzac Square

high point of this walk. Turn left at the top of the stairs and head towards the **Old Windmill ❺**. Established in 1828, this modest structure is Queensland's oldest surviving building. Its dubious effectiveness as a windmill led to the introduction of a treadmill, an instrument of punishment with the power being provided by unruly convicts. Retrace your footsteps back along Edward Street, and turn right to go southwest along Ann Street.

KING GEORGE SQUARE

About 50m/yds from the corner is **Sage on Ann**, see ❷, a breakfast, lunch, and coffee stop where you can eat in or grab something to go. Continue along Ann Street until you reach **King George Square** at the confluence of Ann and Albert streets. **Brisbane City Hall ❻** dominates this expansive public space and hosts the **Museum of Brisbane** (www.museumofbrisbane.com.au; daily 10am–5pm, Fri until 7pm; free), which features displays revealing the history of Brisbane, as well as contemporary art. Take the lift up to City Hall's bell tower for stupendous views; afterwards, stroll south through the square to cross Adelaide Street and walk one block back to Albert Street.

 Queen Street Mall ❼ is pedestrianised between Edward and George streets and hosts a multitude of shopping and eating possibilities (see page 41). For now, continue southwest,

crossing George Street towards the Treasury Building.

WILLIAM STREET

Continue southwest alongside the Italianate **Treasury Building**, which houses a 24-hour casino behind its numerous arches, and turn left down William Street. Stroll through Queens Park with its stern statue of Queen Victoria and pass by the grand Lands Administration Building, now the **Treasury Casino and Hotel** (see page 103). On the opposite side of the road is the **Commissariat Store ❽** (No. 115; Tue–Fri 10am–4pm; free), an 1829 convict-era building housing a museum focusing on Brisbane's earliest beginnings and local Aboriginal history.

PARLIAMENT HOUSE

Cross back to the eastern side of William Street and head southeast to Margaret Street and turn left. Turn right on George Street passing **The Mansions**, six charming three-storey terraced houses, on the way to **Parliament House ❾** (corner George and Alice streets; www.parliament.qld.gov.au; Mon–Fri 9am–4.45; free), where there are on-demand guided tours of the fully restored interior and decorative antiques. Alternatively, observe all the action (or boredom) from the visitors' gallery when parliament sits (see website).

The grand structure of Brisbane's City Hall

Resume your walk south past the lush Botanic Gardens on your left and the **Queensland University of Technology** (QUT) on your right. Soon a sweeping driveway on your right heralds the presence of the serene, creamy-stone **Old Government House** (2 George Street; www.ogh.qut.edu.au; Sun–Fri 10am–4pm; free). Once the home of Queensland's governors, the attractive mansion also houses the exceptional **William Robinson Gallery** (Sun–Fri 10am–4pm), filled with the work of this award-winning Queensland artist.

CITY BOTANIC GARDENS

Cross over George Street, past the QUT Gardens Theatre and enter the **City Botanic Gardens** (daily, 24 hours; free). Originally a convict-worked farm, the gardens were formally laid out in 1855 – now you can explore them (and go much further) by hiring a bike from nearby Bike Obsession (133 Mary Street; www.bikeobsession.com.au; Mon 8am–5.30pm, Tue–Fri 7.30am–5.30pm, Sat 9am–2pm; charge).

Consider pausing at the café for refreshments, then head down the stone steps through rainforest towards the river. At the Riverside Promenade, turn right where you will see a board-walk extending out into the **mangrove forest**. Follow the boardwalk looking for birdlife and read about the significance of the muddy mangrove ecosystem on panels. Re-join the promenade and head north.

EDWARD STREET TO EAGLE STREET

Exit the gardens at Edward Street passing the old **Naval Offices**, now occupied by upmarket boutiques and restaurants, on your right. On the corner with Margaret Street is the **Port Office Hotel**, see ❸, a popular lunch option. Turn right at Margaret Street and then left along Felix Street. At the Mary Street intersection, turn right beside the colonial **Naldham House** . When you reach the anchor beside the eastern wall, turn around. Three small brass plaques on the corner of the building mark the water levels of the 1893, 1896 and 1974 floods. Can't see the 1893 plaque? Look up!

Pass under the shade sails towards the river and the **Eagle Street Pier** complex. Here you'll find more eateries and cafés, plus paddle-steamer cruise boats (www.kookaburrariverqueens.com) and a ferry terminal. If you're looking for a detour, hop on a stubby river ferry from the Eagle Street Pier to Holman Street on Kangaroo Point and check out the charismatic **Story Bridge Hotel**. The ferry ride affords great views of the city and Story Bridge, particularly at night. Turn right outside the Holman Street terminal and follow the riverside walkway

George Street's Mansions *Brisbane City Botanic Gardens*

for 500m/yds as far as Bright Street. Turn left and you will spot the Story Bridge Hotel (see page 121) tucked under the Story Bridge approach ramp.

BACK TO QUEEN STREET MALL

To continue with this route, head west, away from the river, to the intersection of Creek, Eagle and Charlotte streets. Walk southwest along Charlotte Street towards the steps leading up to the beautifully refurbished **St Stephen's Cathedral** (entrance on Elizabeth Street) dating from the 1860s, and the neighbouring **St Stephen's Chapel**, Queensland's first church, built in 1850.

Cross Elizabeth Street in front of the cathedral and take the narrow lane between Brisbane GPO and Newspaper House (now the Manor Apartment Hotel) to emerge on Queen Street with the open plaza of **Post Office Square** opposite. Turn left on Queen Street and cross over Edward Street to enter Queen Street Mall. Pass by the helpful **Brisbane Visitor Information Centre** (Queen Street Mall; tel: 3006 6290; www.visitbrisbane.com. au; Mon–Thu 9am–5.30pm, Fri until 7pm, Sat until 5pm, Sun 10am–5pm) and walk 400m/yds until you reach **Brisbane Arcade** ⓭ on your right. The three storeys of the arcade, which runs through to Adelaide Street, are crammed with tempting elegant tearooms, jewellers and high-end fashion shops.

Food and Drink

① AQUILA CAFFE BAR

82 Eagle St; tel: 3221 2228; www.aquila. net.au; Mon–Thu 6.30am–3pm, Fri until 10pm, Sat 7am–11.30am; $$

Stop in for breakfast and enjoy a cup of freshly-roasted coffee and choose from eggs, acai berry fruit bowls or even a breakfast burger. At lunchtime, pizzas, sandwiches, and pastas fill the menu. Whatever you choose, there is a reason why the place is regularly busy.

② SAGE ON ANN

140 Ann Street; tel: 3221 4471; www. sageonann.com.au; Mon–Thu 6.30am–3.30pm, Fri until 2.30pm; $-$$

Eat in or grab breakfast on the go with options like Turkish eggs or zucchini and asparagus tart. If you are staying for lunch the wild mushroom risotto and beef massaman curry are well worth the price. Home delivery also available.

③ PORT OFFICE HOTEL

Corner Margaret and Edward streets; tel: 3003 4700; www.portofficehotel. com.au; Mon–Sat 11.30am–midnight; $$–$$$

Choose between a good-value bar meal in the casual Marble Bar, tapas in the Fix Bar or elegant dining in the Fix Restaurant. There are wood-fired pizzas, vegetarian dishes and seafood, though the steaks enjoy pride of place.

Enjoying Streets Beach

BRISBANE SOUTH BANK

Filled with entertainment and dining options and wrapped in green parklands, South Bank is Brisbane's playground and Queensland's premier cultural precinct. The area is designed just as much for strolls and relaxation as it is for showcasing its various edifying and recreational attractions.

DISTANCE: 3.75km (2.5 miles) walk; 5km (3-mile) CityCat ride
TIME: A leisurely full day
START: Goodwill Bridge
END: South Bank Wharf 1
POINTS TO NOTE: This walk starts on the CBD side of the Brisbane River, near the City Botanic Gardens, and crosses the river on the car-free Goodwill Bridge. You can return to the CBD by the same bridge, or the solar-powered Kurilpa footbridge, or by Victoria Bridge, but the CityCat (www.translink.com.au/ferries) affords a more relaxing return trip with great views, and delivers you to the Riverside Precinct, a locality crammed with restaurants.

South Bank was developed for the 1988 World Expo, and as such it is an outstanding example of the positive legacy such large public events can bestow on cities. This former industrial wasteland now has something for everyone: bring your bathers for a splash at Streets Beach, your head for heights for a spin on the Wheel of Brisbane, and your sense of adventure for the Gallery of Modern Art.

Begin at the **Goodwill Bridge ❶** on Gardens Point near the southwest corner of the City Botanic Gardens (see page 40), close to the outdoor **Riverstage**. Built in 2001, this bridge takes its name from Brisbane's Goodwill Games held in the same year. A small coffee stand, Brendan's Cafe, serving locally roasted Merlo coffee, is parked on the bridge towards this end.

QUEENSLAND MARITIME MUSEUM

At the other end of the bridge, a tugboat, a warship and a very odd-looking 'lightship' (half-lighthouse, half-ship) announce the **Queensland Maritime Museum ❷** (Stanley Street; www.maritimemuseum.com.au; daily 9.30am–4.30pm, last entry at 3.30pm; charge). Since Dutch explorers landed on Cape York Peninsula in 1606, the sea has shaped Queenslanders' lives and commerce, and this museum focuses on the state's close links with the sea and historical dependence on it.

HMAS Diamantina   *Kurilpa Bridge*

SOUTH BANK

Opposite the museum you will see the entrance to the **Arbour**, a bougainvillea-draped archway of metal tendrils and wire supports. This living art form shelters a path that meanders through the South Bank Parklands as far as the Wheel of Brisbane (see page 44).

Heading northwest along the Arbour you pass between shady picnic grounds and the Boardwalk, the first of the Arbour's several restaurant zones. A small formal garden appears on your right with a statue of Confucius, where the Arbour curves around a cluster of cafés.

Stanley Street Plaza

Where the cafés end, the **Stanley Street Plaza** ❸ begins. A usually quiet public space featuring the **South Bank Visitor Centre** (South Bank House, Corner of Ernest and Stanley Street Plaza; daily 9am–5pm), the plaza comes alive with buskers and market-goers at the weekend as the venue for the **Collective Markets** (www.collectivemarkets.com.au; Fri 5pm–9pm, Sat 10am–9pm, Sun 9am–4pm). Stalls sell all manner of unique items, from craft collectables to chilli sauces, sarongs to sombreros.

Little Stanley Street

Parallel to the plaza and bordering the parklands, Little Stanley Street is packed with bars and quality restaurants offering casual sidewalk dining. Even if you are not yet hungry, check out what's on offer for future reference. The range of cuisine served up is extraordinary, and includes the exotic ambience and Turkish cuisine of **Ahmet's**, see ❶, and modern Vietnamese flavours, served in a communal setting, at Viet De Lites.

Streets Beach to the Wheel of Brisbane

Between Stanley Street Plaza and the river is **Streets Beach** ❹ (daily; free), Australia's only city-bound 'beach'. This man-made lagoon, complete with sandy shore and lifesavers, is a surreal sight with the muddy river and city skyline as a backdrop, but with no waves or dangerous rips and plenty of shady palm trees, it is one of the South Bank's most popular attractions.

North of the beach, the Arbour weaves between clusters of cafés and restaurants and the Suncorp Piazza, a well-used con-

---

Food and Drink

❶ AHMET'S
10/168 Grey Street; tel: 3846 6699; www.ahmets.com; Mon–Thu 11.30am–9pm, Fri–Sun until 10pm; $$
Be transported to a vibrant bazaar in this colourfully atmospheric Turkish restaurant. Attention to detail extends to the dishes, best shared, which are simply delicious. Dive into the dips, but leave room for the spicy lamb *pide* or the delicious *guvec* (casserole). Entry is from both Grey and Little Stanley streets.

Strolling in the South Bank Parklands

cert venue that often also screens sporting events or movies for free. Take the **Rainforest Walk**, where you should spot a water dragon, a striking (yet harmless) lizard. The boardwalk emerges at the intricately carved **Nepalese Pagoda**, constructed for the 1988 World Expo.

Towering almost 60 metres (197ft) above the parklands, the **Wheel of Brisbane** ❺ (www.thewheelofbrisbane. com.au; daily 10am–10pm; charge) is worth a spin. You receive geographical and historical commentary while inside your air-conditioned pod.

QUEENSLAND CULTURAL CENTRE

Much of Queensland's celebration of culture culminates in this assemblage of edifices at the northern end of the South Bank Parklands. As you leave the Wheel of Brisbane, walk north along the Cultural Forecourt. On your left is the **Queensland Performing Arts Centre (QPAC)** ❻ (cor-

ner Grey and Melbourne streets; www. qpac.com.au). With a multitude of theatres, galleries and event spaces, there is always some action here. (Check out www.visitsouthbank.com.au for a full events calendar and detailed information on all attractions and shows, at the QPAC and beyond.)

Turn left to skirt the northern side of QPAC, where lifts and stairs lead to a walkway over Melbourne Street and to the **Queensland Museum** ❼ (corner Grey and Melbourne streets; www.southbank.qm.qld.gov.au; daily 9.30am–5pm; free). This compact, well-laid-out museum succinctly explores Queensland's natural and social history. The Museum Zoo is a creative line-up of stuffed critters where you can compare your own size and physical abilities against members of the animal kingdom. There is also a kid-friendly, hands-on **Sciencentre** (9.30am–5pm; charge), which includes the interactive Sparklab.

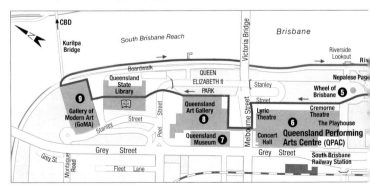

The striking Queensland State Library

Two galleries

Exit the museum where you entered. On your left, the **Whale Mall** reverberates to the recordings of humpback whales; look up to see life-size recreations of these mammals. Straight ahead is a passage heading towards the river and the **Queensland Art Gallery ❽** (Stanley Place; www.qag.qld.gov.au; daily 10am–5pm; free). Head along the passage and find the entrance at the river side of the gallery. Inside, visiting exhibitions accompany indigenous, classical and contemporary art from Australia and abroad, particularly Asia and the Pacific region.

Exit the gallery from the northern side and walk across the elevated plaza over Peel Street towards the **Queensland State Library** (www.slq.qld.gov.au; daily 10am–5pm, to 8pm Mon–Thu). Pass through the centre of the library via the sheltered Knowledge Walk, where you can take advantage of free Wi-Fi.

This ground-floor walkway opens out onto a compound facing the dramatic, glass and steel **Gallery of Modern Art (GoMA) ❾** (same contact details as the Queensland Art Gallery; free). The light-filled modern space showcases contemporary art in a variety of media.

KURILPA BRIDGE

Northeast of GoMA, a lawn descends to the Riverside Boardwalk. To the north, **Kurilpa Bridge**, a sculptural (and controversial) structure of steel masts and cables, with solar-powered LED lighting, is a bridge for pedestrians and cyclists that connects South Bank with the CBD. If your accommodation is in the north of the city this would be the quick way back to base. Otherwise, turn south and follow the boardwalk under Victoria Bridge back to **South Bank 1 ferry wharf** . Here you can catch a CityCat ferry and cruise past Gardens Point to the Riverside Centre.

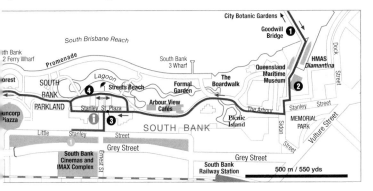

MORETON ISLAND

Moreton Island, just a short ferry trip from Brisbane, delivers a great action-packed day. Four-wheel driving along its vast sandy beaches, plunging into a pristine blue lagoon, snorkelling among shipwrecks, and hand-feeding wild dolphins are just a few of the adventures on offer.

DISTANCE: 50km (31 miles)
TIME: A full day
START/END: Tangalooma Island Resort
POINTS TO NOTE: You will need a 4WD vehicle for this trip, either hired in Brisbane (see page 134) or pre-booked from Tangalooma Resort (see page 135). The route, with stops, will take approximately four hours. The Tangalooma Launch departs at 7am and 10am from Holt Street Wharf (arrive 30 mins early); the resort also offers coach transfers (charge) from city hotels for the 10am launch. Vehicles take the MiCat barge (14 Howard Smith Drive; www.moretonislandadventures.com.au; times change based on the day and season so make sure to check the website. Leaves from the Port of Brisbane. You will need a vehicle access permit (charge) from the MiCat barge or from the Department of National Parks, Recreation, Sports and Racing (NPRSR; http://parks.nprsr.qld.gov.au/permits/). Book accommodation ahead at Tangalooma Resort.

Until the early 1960s, Tangalooma on Moreton Island was one of the world's largest whaling stations, operating from 1951 to 1962, conveniently located close to a narrow deep-water channel, along which about 10,000 humpback whales migrated every year. It was estimated that just 500 humpbacks remained ten years after the station was established. Soon after, the authorities put a stop to all whaling from Tangalooma.

Today, Moreton Island is over 95 percent National Park, and is home to just three small villages and the Tangalooma Island Resort. The latter now occupies the whaling station site and whales remain one Tangalooma's main attractions between June and November, when the humpbacks perform spectacular tail- and flipper-slapping and giant breaches.

TANGALOOMA ISLAND RESORT

Tangalooma Island Resort ❶ (tel: 3637 2000; www.tangalooma.com) offers several dining options, a general store, an ATM, and numerous land- and water-based activities, as well as accommoda-

Tangalooma Island Resort

tion. It is very expensive to hire snorkelling gear, however, so bring your own if possible. Unless you have driven to the island, this is where you will pick up your prebooked 4WD. If you have an early start,

grab some breakfast before you head out from the **Tursiops Restaurant**, see ①, which serves a decent breakfast buffet.

Follow signs to the track that leads onto the beach (there is a no-driving

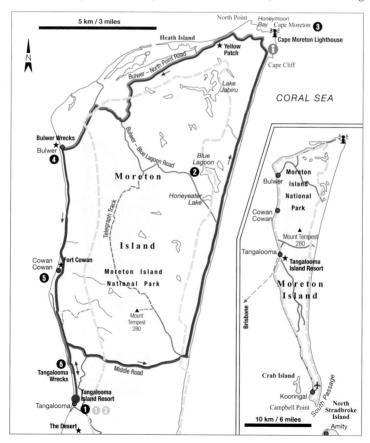

Tangalooma wrecks

zone in front of the resort): from here the drive will be entirely on sand. Note that the best and safest time for beach driving is two hours either side of low tide; tide charts are provided with the island driving permit or the resort vehicle hire. To start, head north just past the Tangalooma Wrecks and turn right onto the inland track, Middle Road.

BLUE LAGOON

After 7km (4 miles) you will reach the eastern side of the island. Turn left and head north along this beautiful 38km (23-mile) stretch of ocean beach. After 8km (5 miles), leave the beach to visit the **Blue Lagoon ❷**, the island's larg-

est freshwater lake, where white sandy shores are lapped by gin-clear water. It is a short stroll from the parking area through heathland down to the lake.

CAPE MORETON

A further 8km (5 miles) north is the tip of **Cape Moreton ❸**, where 360-degree views stretch to the Glass House Mountains, on the mainland, and to North Stradbroke Island. Sit and watch marine wildlife below: turtles, dolphins, sharks, whales, rays and schools of fish are commonly spotted.

The 1.5km (1-mile) walk around the headland winds past the 23-metre (115ft) -high **Cape Moreton Lighthouse**, the oldest operating lighthouse in Queensland. It was built in 1857 with sandstone blocks quarried by 35 prisoners. The unmanned **Moreton Island National Park Information Centre** near the lighthouse provides island history and details on marine life and island wildlife.

Return to the car park and continue west on the inland track, which briefly returns to the beach past **Yellow Patch**, a large dark yellow 'sand blow'. The track then veers inland once again to bypass several tidal lagoons.

BULWER AND COWAN COWAN

Back on the western side of the island, the route passes behind the tiny settlements of Bulwer and Cowan Cowan. (The beaches in front of these two small

---

Bottlenose dolphins

Moreton Bay is home to approximately 550 bottlenose dolphins and, at sunset, Tangalooma is visited by a small pod which frequent the shores to feed, hunt, and play. You are encouraged to learn and identify these endearing creatures by their individual and quite distinctive dorsal fin markings. Anyone can join on the jetty to watch this nightly spectacle; however, if you wish to join in the hand-feeding you must be an overnight guest at the resort or be booked on the resort's extended day tour with dolphin-feeding. You will also need to register at the resort's Marine Education and Conservation Centre from 1–4pm.

Sand tobogganing

Feeding the dolphins

communities are closed to traffic.) On the beach at **Bulwer** ❹, three hulks lie on the sand, having been originally scuttled and placed there in the 1930s to form a safe anchorage for small boats. Some 5.5km (3.5 miles) further south, **Cowan Cowan** ❺ is the site of Fort Cowan, an old navy signal station that was Brisbane's first line of defence during World War II.

TANGALOOMA WRECKS

It is only a short drive now along the beach to one of the island's most recognisable landmarks – the **Tangalooma Wrecks** ❻. In total, 15 former hard-working ships that once sailed all around Australia have been scuttled here to form a small-craft anchorage. The *Maryborough* was the first to be scuttled in July 1963. The wrecks are perfect for snorkelling and scuba-diving. Guided snorkelling trips, are offered by Tangalooma Dive & Watersports.

TANGALOOMA ACTIVITIES

Returning to Tangalooma Island Resort, thrill-seekers can chose from a range of afternoon activities, including quadbike rides in the dunes, kayaking, helicopter flights, parasailing, and seasonal whale-watching cruises. The **Desert Safari Tour** (three daily, 1.5 hours duration; charge) includes a 4WD bus tour through the bush to the "desert", which is in fact a 42ha (100-acre) sand blow. The huge dunes are the venue for **sand tobogganing**; a flimsy piece of waxed board is all you need to fly down at speeds of about 60kph (40mph).

The resort has a couple of good (seasonal) restaurants including the **Beach Café**, see ❷, with two new spots, **Fire and Stone,** offering Sichuan Chinese and modern Australian respectively.

A 4WD hired from Tangalooma will need to be returned by 5pm. There is a late afternoon launch back to the mainland, but a better option is to stay for dolphin-feeding at sunset, and return to Brisbane on a later launch.

Food and Drink

❶ TURSIOPS RESTAURANT

Tangalooma Island Resort; tel: 3410 6000; www.tangalooma.com; daily 7.30am–9.30am in season (check prior to visit); \$\$\$

Casual buffet fare is offered at this spot, which prides itself on a monster breakfast, but also offers lunch daily and dinner on Saturdays.

❷ BEACH CAFÉ

Tangalooma Island Resort; tel: 3410 6000; swww.tangalooma.com; Daily 11.30am–9pm; \$\$

This ultra-casual beachside café offers pizzas, pastas, burgers, salads and a delicious cold seafood platter, as well as children's meals. You'll get to enjoy the views while you dine.

Enjoying Noosa Main Beach

SUNSHINE COAST

Discover natural beauty and charming settlements by leaving the highway to pass through the eerie Glass House Mountains and remnant rainforests on the way to the ridge–top villages of Maleny and Montville, before descending to the chic beachside resort of Noosa.

DISTANCE: 170km (102 miles)
TIME: A full day
START: Brisbane
END: Noosa National Park
POINTS TO NOTE: You will need a car for this full-day adventure. If you start by 8am, you will be able to fit everything in with plenty of stops, but there is so much to see and so much worth doing on the Sunshine Coast that, if time permits, stretching this route out into a two- or even three-day excursion. If you time your trip so you pass through Eumundi on a Wednesday or Saturday, try to catch the popular Eumundi Markets.

The Sunshine Coast is a glorious stretch of coastline extending about 120km (72 miles) from Bribie Island in the south to Rainbow Beach, near Fraser Island, in the north. Compared to the Gold Coast, commercial development is more restrained; though there are still high-rise towers and shopping malls, you are never too far away from a peaceful expanse of golden beach. Noosa is the jewel in the coastal

crown, an unlikely encapsulation of luxury, hedonism and natural beauty that rarely fails to charm visitors. Back from the beach, the rolling green hills of the hinterland are peppered with gorgeous villages and mysterious volcanic mountains.

GLASS HOUSE MOUNTAINS

Head north from Brisbane on the Bruce Highway for approximately 56km (34 miles) and turn left at The Glasshouse Mountains Tourist Drive, also known as the Steve Irwin Way since the death of 'The Crocodile Hunter'. This is where you will catch your first really good glimpses of the **Glass House Mountains ❶**. These unusual volcanic plugs are the remains of lava-belching volcanoes that violently issued from the earth some 20 million years ago. The craggy, eroded peaks in the eponymous national park (see www.nprsr.qld.gov.au) offer impressive walking tracks to panoramic lookouts, while the well-drained slopes of rich volcanic soil around the mountains are ideal for growing pineapples, which are sold by the bucket load at roadside stalls, along with

The atmospheric Glass House Mountains

avocados, macadamia nuts and other produce.

AUSTRALIA ZOO

About 2km (1.25 miles) past Beerwah, a sign directs you to **Australia Zoo ❷** (Steve Irwin Way, Beerwah; www.australia zoo.com.au; daily 9am–5pm; charge). This started out as a small reptile park in the 1970s, created by Bob and Lyn Irwin, but thanks to his irrepressible character and antics with dangerous animals, most notably crocodiles, their son, Steve 'The Crocodile Hunter' Irwin, turned it into a world-renowned zoo. Steve was tragically killed by a stingray in 2006, but his legacy of hands-on conservation continues at the zoo in spite of allegations in 2015 – since dismissed – of the mistreatment of animals. Visitors should exercise their own judgment. Living within natural Australian and recreated Asian habitats, there are numerous mammals, birds and reptiles housed here. Bus tours from Brisbane and

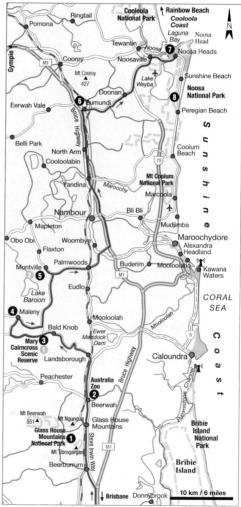

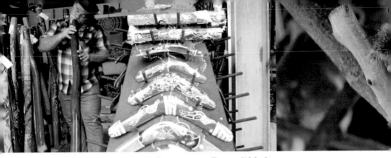

Boomerangs at Eumundi Markets

the Sunshine Coast are also available if you want to come back.

At Landsborough, turn left and drive up the hill, following the signs and the winding road towards Maleny. As you climb, remember to check out the splendid views of patchwork farms and the coast far to the east, which are gradually revealed. There are many designated spots to stop the car, whip out the camera and capture the countryside, so take advantage of them.

MARY CAIRNCROSS SCENIC RESERVE

After 9km (5.5 miles), turn left at Cairncross Corner off the main Maleny road, to **Mary Cairncross Scenic Reserve ❸** (www.mary-cairncross.com.au). The reserve protects a remnant of the magnificent subtropical rainforest that once covered these ranges. There are easy trails (including some that are wheelchair-accessible) through the rainforest, offering unobstructed views of the cultivated valleys, rugged Glass House Mountains and distant coastline. For a late breakfast or early lunch, head to the delightful **Mountain View Café**, see ❶.

MALENY

Continue on the same road for 9km (5.5 miles), following the signposted tourist drive, which loops north to the hill township of **Maleny ❹** – a picturesque country town with beautiful colonial architecture occupied by new-age shops, galleries and craft outlets. Many talented artists and craftspeople have made this their home, and you may just find that something special here that is genuinely Australian and original.

MONTVILLE

Head east on the Maleny–Landsborough Road for 4km (2.5 miles) before taking a left turn to Montville, which lies around 10km (6 miles) further north. Again you will enjoy spectacular ridge-top vistas en route, plus a few glimpses of scenic Lake Baroon. **Montville ❺**, visually even more of a chocolate-box town than Maleny, is ornamented with determinedly quaint shops offering all manner of arts and crafts. The main street is well worth a wander, with numerous options for eating and drinking, such as **The Edge Restaurant**, see ❷.

EUMUNDI

Head east again for a further 15km (9 miles) to the Bruce Highway, and then turn left towards Nambour to reach Eumundi after 26km (16 miles). Yet another charming hinterland town, **Eumundi ❻** is decorated with contemporary artwork by local artists; mingling with the historic buildings are plenty of shops and cafés. But it is the renowned markets (Memorial Drive, Eumundi; www.eumundimarkets.com.au; Wed 8am–1.30pm and Sat 7am–2pm) that have put Eumundi on the map. Some

A koala at Australia Zoo   *Surfers at Noosa Main Beach*

20,000 people – both locals and visitors – have been flocking here twice a week, for 40 years, to peruse hundreds of stalls selling local produce, arts and crafts and crystals. From Eumundi, it is 21km (13 miles) northeast via Route 12 to the coast at Noosa.

NOOSA

Noosa includes Noosaville, set back on the Noosa River; Noosa Junction; and Sunshine Beach, but for most people the name really refers to the compact area called **Noosa Heads ❼**.

Located on the sandy shore of Laguna Bay at the mouth of the river and overlooked by a ruggedly natural headland, the main Noosa 'strip' is **Hastings Street**, where the chintziest shops, finest restaurants and beautiful people all come together. All your information and booking needs are met by the **Noosa Visitor Centre** (Hastings Street; www.visitnoosa.com.au; daily 9am–5pm). Directly in front of Hastings Street is **Noosa Heads Main Beach**, where you can surf or just enjoy messing about on the beach.

Around Noosa Heads

Other places to explore locally include **Noosa National Park ❽** south of town, and **Noosa North Shore**, across the river. The **Queensland Parks and Wildlife Service Information Centre** in Noosa National Park is just a few minutes' walk from Hastings Street, and from there you can access walking trails where you might spot koalas and admire spectacular views of the Pacific Ocean and Sunshine Coast. Noosa North Shore is the start of the remote **Cooloola Coast**, which stretches right up to **Rainbow Beach**. It is accessed by a ferry near Tewantin and is best explored by 4WD, but even without a 4WD, horse and camel riding can be organised; ask for more details at the Noosa Visitor Centre.

Food and Drink

❶ MOUNTAIN VIEW CAFÉ AT MARY CAIRNCROSS SCENIC RESERVE

148 Mountain View Road, Maleny; tel: 5499 9180; http://mountainviewcafe.com.au; Mon–Fri 8.30am–4.30pm, Sat–Sun 8am–5pm; $

Breakfast on sourdough bread, eggs and bacon (at least until 11.30am) or lunch on variations of BLTs, burgers and salads. The coffee is organic and fairtrade, as befits the natural setting.

❷ THE EDGE RESTAURANT

The Mayfield Centre, 127–133 Main Street, Montville; tel: 5442 9344; www.theedgerestaurant.net.au; Daily 8.30am–4pm; $$

If you can take your eyes off the spectacular hinterland views that stretch away to the Pacific Ocean, you will find a light and seasonal Modern Australian menu of pasta dishes, salads, steaks and seafood here, in dishes such as salt-and-pepper prawns.

NORTH STRADBROKE ISLAND

North Stradbroke has long been Brisbane's favourite escape. Seemingly endless white-sand beaches, freshwater lagoons and wilderness walks will delight back-to-nature types, and for those who'd prefer not to go 'bush', there are also plenty of options for pampered relaxation and fine dining.

DISTANCE: 71km (43 miles), not including drive on Main Beach
TIME: A full day
START/END: Dunwich
POINTS TO NOTE: A 4WD is needed for the full route to be explored, although a conventional car is fine if you plan on leaving out the beach driving. Vehicle ferries and water taxis access the island from Cleveland Ferry Terminal, 35km (21 miles) southeast of Brisbane CBD; to catch a 9am ferry, be sure to leave Brisbane by 7.45am. On some days the ferry departs as early as 5.45am; the crossing takes 45 minutes. Ferry operators include Stradbroke Ferries (www.stradbrokeferries.com.au). You must book in advance, and the ferry company can arrange your beach access (driving) permit. Along with the permit, you will get a tide chart.

North Stradbroke, or 'Straddie' to the locals, is an island of immense natural beauty and, at 38km (23 miles) long and 11km (7 miles) wide, it is the world's second-largest sand island, after Fraser Island (see page 65). It has been home to the Nunukul, Nughie and Goenpul peoples, who know it as Minjerribah, for many thousands of years – artefacts and evidence of Aboriginal settlement date back over 20,000 years. European settlement stretches back a more modest 185 years, to a time when a shipping pilot station was established at Amity Point. Today's small, permanent population of approximately 3,000 swells considerably at weekends and during public holidays.

DUNWICH

The small fishing township of **Dunwich ❶** was used variously by the Europeans as a convict outstation, a Catholic mission, a quarantine station and a benevolent institution. A Heritage Trail leads walkers around the many buildings remaining from this period and winds through convict relics and graves dating right back to those shipwrecked in the 1800s. You can find advice, services and information about

Cylinder Beach

what's new by visiting the official tourist information website for the island (https://stradbrokeisland.com).

Your first stop should be the **North Stradbroke Island Historical Museum** (15–17 Welsby Street; www.stradbrokemuseum.com; Tue–Sat 10am–2pm, Sun 11am–3pm; charge), housed in an original dormitory of the benevolent institution, offers an impressive display of photographs and items retrieved from shipwrecks, as well as information about Aboriginal and pioneer settlements, and the sand-mining industry.

POINT LOOKOUT

From Dunwich, drive 19km (12 miles) northeast to the township of **Point Lookout ❷**. Named by James Cook in 1770, this is Queensland's most easterly point and is one of the best land-based vantage points to witness the acrobatic antics of magnificent humpback whales. Flipper-slapping, tail-waving and mighty breaching leaps that result in explosive splashdowns can all be witnessed as the whales pass by here from June to November, on their annual migration north. The

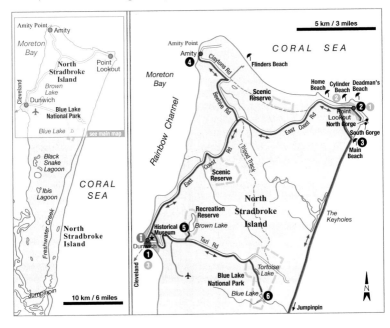

Prawn trawlers off North Stradbroke Island

whales will have been feeding all summer in the rich waters of Antarctica, and now head for their calmer calving grounds in the Coral Sea.

The rocky headland shelters several excellent beaches, such as Deadman's (unpatrolled but good for exploring rock pools), Cylinder (a patrolled surf beach, ideal for families), Home (unpatrolled) and Flinders (unpatrolled, 4WDs allowed).

Do what Cook certainly did not do and enjoy a refreshing morning tea break at the **Oceanic Gelati & Coffee Bar**, see ①, and then cross the road to start the spectacular **North Gorge Walk** (the path begins beside the public toilet block). It's only a little over 1km (0.65 mile) and the views are superb. As the pathway clings to the edge of the coast, keep your eyes on the water and watch out for humpback whales. Often it's possible to spot large pods of dolphins, graceful manta rays, sharks and turtles, all swimming freely in the sparkling blue waters below. In places you can walk out onto the rocky coastline to sit and watch the marine wildlife show and admire the powerful waves crashing into the shore. Further along, the walk ventures onto **South Gorge** and then the sweeping expanse of Main Beach comes into view. As the path ends and heads towards the road, turn right and you will discover that you are only a short distance away from your starting point.

The views from Point Lookout are truly sublime, and to continue the experience over lunch, drive back along the road you came in on to the **Stradbroke Island Beach Hotel & Spa Resort**, see ②, known to locals simply as the Straddie Pub. In whale-watching season you can sit and eat your fresh fish and chips here while watching whales breach and splash below.

MAIN BEACH

Just to the west of the Straddie Pub there is a turnoff to the south onto George Nothling Drive, with signposts indicating access to **Main Beach** ③. (Before heading down this way, consult your tide chart, as beach driving is best an hour or so either side of low tide and is prohibited an hour either side of high tide.) This amazing stretch of pristine white beach is legendary with Stradbroke regulars. Surfers rise to the challenge on these waves, fishermen cast into the deep 'gutters' (channels between the breaks), pulling in dinner, and you can easily find a patch of lonely beach to comb.

At the right time, it is possible to drive the entire 34km (21-mile) length of beach to **Jumpinpin**, the sea channel between North and South Stradbroke islands, which were once connected.

AMITY POINT

It is a 12km (7.5 mile) drive west from Point Lookout to **Amity** ④, a down-to-earth fishing village on the island's northwestern tip. A pilot station was established here in 1825 and Amity became the main access

Taking a canoe to the beach

On Amity's jetty at sunset

point for boats coming from Brisbane over the next 150 years. These days, families come here for the beachside camping, calm waters, good fishing and safe swimming (although, it's worth noting, Amity Point was the scene of a fatal shark attack in 2006, with the victim taken in waist-deep water).

BROWN AND BLUE LAKES

From Amity Point, retrace your drive back out onto the East Coast Road and turn right for Dunwich. If you have time to spare before your return ferry, **Brown Lake ❺** is only 4km (2.5 miles) east of Dunwich, and it is worth taking a glimpse at this perched lake, part of the island's amazing freshwater lake system. The water is stained tea-brown by the surrounding trees, reeds and organic matter, but you can take a refreshing swim in its cool embrace, or wander the walking trail around its shore. Alternatively, **Blue Lake ❻** is 10km (6 miles) east of Dunwich (accessible by a conventional car), and from the car park it is a further 3km (1.65-mile) walk (approximately 30 minutes). The gin-like water laps clean white sand, turning a rich blue colour as the lake deepens. Wildlife abounds, especially in the early morning or late afternoon, and it's common to spot swamp wallabies and sand goannas.

Head back to Dunwich to catch the ferry back to Brisbane, and if there is time for an afternoon tea stop, visit the **Island Fruit Barn**, see ❸, in town.

Food and Drink

❶ OCEANIC GELATI & COFFEE BAR

19 Mooloomba Road, Point Lookout; tel: 3415 3222; Mon–Fri 9.30am–5pm, Sat–Sun from 8.30am; $

Choose from a great range of fruit juices, smoothies, gelato and coffee. Especially good is the *affogato* – espresso poured over ice cream.

❷ STRADBROKE ISLAND BEACH HOTEL & SPA RESORT

East Coast Road, Point Lookout; tel: 3409 8188; www.stradbrokehotel.com.au; daily 7am–11am, 12pm–3pm, 5.30pm–9pm; $$$

Overlooking the beach, the bistro and beer garden of the 'Straddie Pub' offer an excellent choice of local seafood, including Straddie prawns and beer-battered coral trout, plus succulent steaks, pizzas, and meals for little 'nippers'.

❸ ISLAND FRUIT BARN

16 Bingle Road, Dunwich; tel: 3409 9125; www.islandfruitbarn.com; daily 7.30am–3.30pm; $$

This atypical fruit barn adds value to its array of seasonal fruits and vegetables by tempting travellers with fresh salads, organic fruit smoothies, delicious cakes and decent coffee.

Apartment buildings in Surfers Paradise

GOLD COAST

Queensland's Gold Coast is not just a surfer's paradise. On this driving route you can certainly catch waves, but also explore the region's golden shores and glittering malls, take to its high-rise towers, and discover its quiet corners and natural charm.

DISTANCE: 102km (61 miles)
TIME: A full day
START: Brisbane
END: Currumbin Wildlife Sanctuary
POINTS TO NOTE: Don't forget your swimming gear, hat and sunscreen. If time permits, extend your stay to fully enjoy the theme parks, surf and plethora of natural and man-made attractions this area offers. You can also combine this route with Route 7. The Gold Coast is easily accessed by bus or train-and-bus combination from Brisbane, and there are bus connections directly from Brisbane Airport. The Gold Coast also has its own airport at Coolangatta, 25km (15.5 miles) south of Surfers Paradise.

The post-war boom of the late 1940s saw this area wake to a future full of potential, and opportunists have continued to make it their home. The hedonistic lifestyle and garishness that characterises the high-rise section of The Strip culminates in Surfers Paradise, Queensland's answer to Miami or Ipanema. However, the Gold Coast is not just about stretches of golden beaches backed by skyscrapers, a concentration of colourful theme parks and a culture of conspicuous commercialism. As you move along the coast away from 'Paradise', you'll discover more natural beauty. The surf beaches – particularly Burleigh Heads, set in national parkland – are strikingly gorgeous.

MAIN BEACH

From Brisbane, drive southeast for 64km (40 miles) on the Southeast Freeway (Route 3), which becomes the Pacific Motorway (M1). You will pass signs to several theme parks (see page 26), as most are concentrated at the northwestern end of the coastal strip, just off the motorway. At Helensvale, turn off at Exit 62 onto the Gold Coast Highway and drive for 13km (8 miles) to **Main Beach ❶**. This has long been a favoured spot for the stylish and wealthy, and those who enjoy chic boutiques and being seen in trendy cafés.

The view from Skypoint

Soaking up the sun on Main Beach

The Spit is a 3km (2-mile) sandbar running north of Main Beach, separating the Broadwater from the Coral Sea. Head along Seaworld Drive where, on the left you will find the **Marina Mirage** (www.marinamirage.com.au; daily 10am–6pm), a luxury yacht marina combined with an upmarket shopping complex of fashion boutiques, cafés and restaurants. Have a morning brew at **Julius Meinl Coffee Cup**, see ❶, then drop in to admire the opulence of the **Palazzo Versace Hotel** next door, or window-shop the classy boutiques.

Also adjacent to Marina Mirage is **Mariners Cove (Fisherman's Wharf)**, with yet more dining options as well as numerous companies offering watersport activities from fishing to jet boating. Further along the Spit is **Sea World**.

SURFER'S PARADISE

Continue south on the Gold Coast Highway for 3km (2 miles) to **Surfers Paradise** ❷, the flashy pendant on this stretch of coastline bling. Epitomising the quirky and superficial culture of Surfers is the continued presence of the strip's famous 'Meter Maids'. First introduced in 1965 to put a positive spin on the fact that parking meters had been installed on the tourist strip, the 'maids' are young women clad

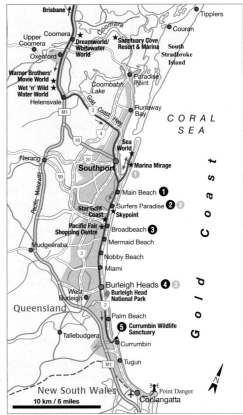

Surfers Paradise is a modern beach town

in tiaras and gold bikinis, who walk the streets putting coins into meters. They have long attracted worldwide attention and, despite the controversial and anachronistic portrayal of women they promote, are a part Gold Coast 'culture' that doesn't seem to be going anywhere.

But it was the surf that first lured people to these beaches, and it's the surf that provides the prime attraction, so factor in some time to enjoy it.

When you're done with swimming, surfing or just lying about, check out **Skypoint** (Q1 Surfers Paradise Boulevard; www.skypoint.com.au, Sun–Thur 7.30am–9pm, Fri–Sat until 10pm; charge), one of the Gold Coast's essential attractions. Here you will ascend to Level 77, at 322m (1,056ft) the Gold Coast's tallest attraction, for breathtaking 360-degree views that extend up and down the coast from Brisbane to Byron Bay.

For lunch beside the ocean with a dose of Aussie beach culture, walk a few blocks south along the shoreline to the **BMD Northcliffe Surf Club**, see ❷.

BROADBEACH

A short 2km (1.25 miles) hop south is **Broadbeach** ❸, a slightly less frenetic and more family friendly town than Surfers, but still a zone of residential towers, shopping malls and tempting eateries. If you haven't had enough retail therapy, turn right into Hooker Boulevard and stop at **Pacific Fair Shopping Centre** (www.pacificfair.com.au; Mon–Sat 9am–7pm, Thu until 9pm, Sun until 6pm), one of the largest shopping malls in the Southern Hemisphere and jam-packed with fashion stores. Across the road, just a few minutes' walk away, is the Star Gold Coast (www.star.com.au/goldcoast/casino; daily). With several restaurants and multiple bars, plus the gaming tables and machines, there's no end to the ways you can lighten your wallet here.

BURLEIGH HEADS

A further 8km (5 miles) south brings you to **Burleigh Heads** ❹, the Gold Coast's

---

Learn to surf

The Gold Coast is one of the great surfing meccas of the world, with excellent beach breaks all along the coast, so it makes sense to grab both a board and an instructor to give the sport a try. Beginner lessons are generally two hours long, and start with honing your technique on the sand before heading to the water for the exhilaration of standing up on your board for the first time. Several surf schools are located up and down the coast. At the Cheyne Horan School of Surf (The Esplanade, Surfers Paradise; www.cheynehoran.com.au), the former world surfing champion and his small team of instructors offer daily beginner classes at 10am and 2pm, and they guarantee you'll be standing and surfing after your first lesson!

Currumbin Wildlife　　　　　　　*Bright lights at night from Skypoint*

premier family destination. Here the beaches are backed by beautiful parkland, and you can sit under beachside pines and palms while watching the surfers take on some of Australia's best waves. A block back from the beach, have yourself a big feed at **The Little Plate**, see ❶.

Burleigh Head National Park (veer left along Goodwin Terrace as you come into Burleigh Heads) is fantastic for views. If you have a spare hour and you're keen to stretch your legs, the 2.5km (1.5-mile) **Ocean View Circuit** leads around the rocky headland from Tallebudgera Creek to the southern edge of Burleigh Heads Township.

CURRUMBIN WILDLIFE SANCTUARY

Six kilometres (4 miles) south of Burleigh Heads is one of the Gold Coast's oldest tourist attractions, **Currumbin Wildlife Sanctuary** ❺ (28 Tomewin Street, Currumbin; www.cws.org.au; daily 8am–5pm; charge), which continues to delight kids of all ages with interactive wildlife displays. At the time of writing, the sanctuary had ceased its nocturnal tours, but look out for new initiatives in the future. From Currumbin head back to Brisbane, about 100km (63 miles) away on the Pacific Motorway, or continue the tour of the Gold Coast Hinterland (see page 62).

Food and Drink

❶ JULIUS MEINL COFFEE CUP

74 Seaworld Drive, Main Beach; tel: 405 020 009; https://jmcoffeecup.com.au; daily 9am–5pm; $–$$
If you can't resist the smells wafting from the doorway, sit down surrounded by the delicious aroma and take the time to enjoy a premium cup of Austrian coffee to start your day.

❷ BMD NORTHCLIFFE SURF CLUB

At Garfield Terrace and Thornton Street, Surfers Paradise; tel: 5539 8091; www.bmdnorthcliffe. com.au; daily 7.30am–9pm, Bar open until midnight; $$
Beachside surf lifesaving clubs are iconic in Australia, and at this one you can watch the action on the beach while enjoying a casual and extensive menu that includes everything from burgers, baguettes, sandwiches, pasta and pizza to chargrilled meats and seafood dishes.

❸ THE LITTLE PLATE

11/3 Deodar drive, Burleigh Heads; tel: 0499 724 303; www.thelittleplate.com.au; Mon, Weds–Sun 5.30pm–10pm, Sun also 12pm–3pm; $$
With a relaxed attitude to everything from shared plates to opening hours, this informal and friendly little restaurant is serious only about one thing: the quality of its food, which is served from a brilliantly varied menu offering tasty titbits from right around the world cuisine. Hard to go past the local seafood, though, the squid is sublime.

Walking in Lamington National Park

GOLD COAST HINTERLAND

Behind the cement–and–glass forests of the Gold Coast is a verdant hinterland of rugged ranges sheltering villages, plunging waterfalls and nature retreats. Much of this stunning landscape is protected in three National Parks: Tamborine, Lamington and Springbrook.

DISTANCE: 170km (102 miles)
TIME: Two days
START: Oxenford turnoff
END: Springbrook National Park
POINTS TO NOTE: This is a driving route. From Brisbane, head southeast for about 60km (36 miles) on the Southeast Freeway (Route 3), which becomes the Pacific Motorway (M1), exiting at Oxenford. If you are starting this route from the Gold Coast, either head north along the Gold Coast Highway and the Pacific Motorway to exit at Oxenford, or access the Pacific Motorway at Nerang. From the Oxenford exit off the motorway, head west for about 2km (1.25 miles) before turning right onto the Tamborine–Oxenford Road and following a 19km (11.5-mile) route that takes you to Eagle Heights.

About an hour's drive from either Brisbane or the Gold Coast high-rises is a realm of lush rainforests, waterfalls and glorious natural vistas. The bush that forms the Gold Coast's green backdrop is in stark contrast to the hype of the coastal strip and is the ideal hangover cure after sampling the party lifestyle. The rugged ranges that challenged the pioneers and cedar-getters now embrace spas, wineries, cheese factories and craft stalls. There are also several 'islands' of native bush protected in National Parks offering idyllic nature-focused retreats.

MOUNT TAMBORINE

The winding road from the **Oxenford turnoff** on the Pacific Motorway ascends for 19km (11.5 miles) through a mixture of native bush and rolling pastures to Eagle Heights with sweeping views of the Gold Coast, its hinterland and the ocean beyond. This mountain oasis comprises the three close-knit heritage communities of Mount Tamborine, North Tamborine and Eagle Heights, and is collectively referred to as **Mount Tamborine**. The **Visitor Information Centre** (Doughty Park, Main Western Road, North Tamborine; www.tamborinemtncc.org.au; daily 9.30am–3.30pm, Sat–Sun until 4pm) can provide maps of the local roads, bushwalks and National Parks.

Panoramic views

Rapids in Lamington National Park

Eagle Heights

Gallery Walk in **Eagle Heights ❶** is the mountain community's shopping precinct and is filled with an array of touristy craft shops, galleries and alfresco eateries. For morning tea (or a piece of morning fudge), head to **Granny Macs Store**, see ❶. Continue to the end of Gallery Walk (it turns into Long Road) and turn left into Curtis Road. At the end of this road there is access to a beautiful 900m/yd rainforest walk to **Cedar Creek Falls**, part of **Tamborine National Park ❷**. If you are extending your stay there are many other great walks in this National Park that comprises 14 separate parcels of land, one of which, **Witches Falls**, was Queensland's first National Park. Well worth a detour while you're here is Australia's smallest operating pot distillery, **Tamborine Mountain Distillery** (87–91 Beacon Road, North Tamborine; www.tamborinemountaindistillery.com; daily 10am–4pm), which has won international awards for its liqueurs, schnapps, vodkas and fruit brandies, flavoured by the amazing range and quality of fruit grown on Mount Tamborine's rich volcanic soils. There's a delightful organic farm and distillery, and they do cellar-door sales.

LAMINGTON NATIONAL PARK

From North Tamborine take the Tamborine Mountain Road south to Mount Tamborine and continue towards Canungra, turning left at the Canungra–Nerang crossroads and right a little further on at the Beechmont/Binna Burra road. You have now descended into the **Coomera River Valley** and are climbing the opposite ridge to the hilltop village of Beechmont. Turn right here for the 10km (6-mile) drive to **Binna Burra Mountain Lodge** (see page 106), 800m (2,600ft) above sea level, in the World Heritage–listed 20,000ha (50,000-acre) **Lamington National Park ❸**. The lodge was

Natural Bridge, at Springbrook National Park

the first resort in the region to gain official ecotourism accreditation and offers a unique chance to escape everyday life.

Detailed walking maps and park brochures are available at the **National Parks and Wildlife Information Centre** (https://findapark.npsr.qld.gov.au/parks/lamington), just before the Lodge. The **Rainforest Circuit** is an easy 30-minute walk, while the short **Bellbird Lookout Walk** offers excellent views of the Numinbah Valley, which used to be the habitat of the valuable hoop pine and the red cedar, the harvesting of which led to the establishment of the first European settlement here, which in turn ultimately resulted in the clearing of the valley.

SPRINGBROOK NATIONAL PARK

Return down the same route via Beechmont, but turn right close to the bottom of the hill and take the Nerang–Murwillumbah road (Route 97) via Advancetown. This takes you up the scenic Numinbah Valley to the **Natural Bridge** (also known as the Natural Arch) section of **Springbrook National Park ④**. About 25km (15 miles) from the Advancetown turn-off, you will find the Natural Bridge car park. A 1km (0.65-mile) circular walk brings you to this peculiar formation where **Cave Creek** stream plunges through the eroded roof of an underground basalt cavern; you can enter further down the pathway to view the waterfall. Access to the Cave Creek area is restricted due to serious accidents that have occurred in the past, so check before you go. For more waterfalls, make the detour to take the 4km (2.5-mile) **Purlingbrook Falls** circuit walk through the Springbrook Plateau section of the national park, which is rich in natural beauty, bushwalks and waterfalls. Allow two to three hours to do the circuit walk, which starts from the Gwongorella picnic area. To get there, return down the Nerang–Murwillumbah road and, after 11km (6.5 miles), turn right and right again onto the Springbrook Road (Route 99). The Dancing Waters Cafe next to the car park is a good bet for a snack or a light lunch.

From Natural Bridge it is 100km (60 miles) to Brisbane. Head back down the Nerang–Murwillumbah Road, continue straight on the Beaudesert–Nerang Road, following signs to Nerang. At Nerang you will merge onto the Pacific Motorway for the 71km (42.5-mile) trip back to Brisbane.

Kingfisher Bay Resort

FRASER ISLAND

This three-day 4WD adventure takes you through an extraordinary wilderness where flourishing rainforests, pristine freshwater lakes and streams, and desert-like sand dunes are accessed via long, lonely highways of sand. This is the world's largest sand island and an area of rare beauty.

DISTANCE: 157km (94 miles), mostly on day two
TIME: Three days
START/END: Kingfisher Bay
POINTS TO NOTE: For the 12.30pm ferry to the island from River Heads, 300km (186 miles) north of Brisbane, pre-book a ticket (www.fraserislandferry.com.au) for the Kingfisher Bay Ferry and leave the city by 7am. Take the Bruce Highway to the Maryborough exit and follow signs to Hervey Bay and River Heads. Collect your ticket at least 20 minutes prior to departure. You can also fly to Hervey Bay. River Heads has a café and store to buy picnic supplies for lunch. Hire a 4WD vehicle in Brisbane, Hervey Bay or at Kingfisher Bay Resort. A beach-driving permit must be obtained, either from Queensland Parks and Wildlife Service (http://parks.nprsr.qld.gov.au) or from the ferry before you board.

Fraser Island was listed as a Unesco World Heritage Site in 1992, an act that recog-nised its natural wonders, including rare dune, lake and forest ecosystems. A great variety of plant species on the island grow entirely on sand and range from coastal heath to mangrove forests, swamps and subtropical rainforests.

Evidence suggests that the indige-nous Butchulla people (now living on the mainland) occupied these parts for more than 5,500 years. Their name for the island was K'gari, which fittingly means paradise. Although logging and sand mining become major industries after European discovery, they were halted a couple of decades ago, allowing Fraser Island to recover its natural state.

One of Fraser Island's biggest attrac-tions are its dingoes. As hunters and scavengers, however, they are wild and unpredictable, and have been known to attack humans, so keep all food secure and do not leave rubbish or scraps lying around.

KINGFISHER BAY RESORT

From River Heads on the mainland, it takes 50 minutes to reach **Kingfisher**

4WD tours of Fraser Island are very popular

Bay Resort ❶. This, the larger of the island's two resorts, nestles on the edge of the Great Sandy Strait on Fraser Island's western shore. It is a multi-award-winning ecotourism resort with accommodation designed to conserve energy, minimise waste and blend with the surrounding bush.

LAKE MCKENZIE

On the first afternoon, take to the island's inland bush tracks, following signs from the resort, to drive 12km (7 miles) southeast to Lake McKenzie. From now on you will be driving on sand tracks, generally only wide enough for one vehicle, so it is important to be vigilant for oncoming 4WDs. The drive time will depend on the condition of the track: if conditions are dry and rough, vehicles may become bogged and cause delays to your journey. A good run from Kingfisher Bay to Lake McKenzie will take 45 minutes, but it could take double that. Remember to pack water and food, as there are no facilities en route.

At the end of your winding drive through lush vegetation, **Lake McKenzie ❷** will dazzle you with its translucent blue water, washing above pure white sand. Sitting 100m (330ft) above sea level and covering more than 150ha (370 acres), this perched lake is not fed by streams or groundwater but contains only rainwater filtered by the sand, making the water so pure it can support very little life.

Wanggoolba Creek

Rusty remnants of the Maheno

Take the time to swim and laze on the soft sandy shores, before returning to Kingfisher Resort for sunset cocktails out on the jetty, or a stroll along the beach before a buffet-style dinner where the focus is on locally sourced ingredients at **Maheno Restaurant**, see ❶.

CENTRAL STATION

The order in which you do things on the second day will be determined by tide times. The best beach driving will be at low tide or within two hours either side. The following itinerary has been based on low tide happening in the middle of the day.

After breakfast, depart by 8am for the 14km (8.5-mile) drive southeast to Central Station. From the resort, take the first sign that says Lake McKenzie. At the next junction, take a right turn onto Bennett Road, follow for approximately 6km (3.5 miles), then turn left at the next junction.

Originally an old logging depot, **Central Station** ❸ crouches under towering bunya pines and is now the starting point for many pretty walks into the surrounding areas. The **Pile Valley Circuit Walk** is a 4.5km (3-mile) boardwalk around **Wanggoolba Creek**, an astonishingly clear and pristine stream. The walk then winds through awesome satinay trees that grow to more than 60m (197ft).

Return to your vehicle and continue 8km (5 miles) east, following the signs to Eurong Beach Resort.

SEVENTY-FIVE MILE BEACH

The small village of **Eurong** ❹ has a resort and limited facilities, but you can buy petrol and a small selection of groceries. There is one restaurant, **McKenzie's Restaurant**, see ❷, and a bakery, which is a good place to buy a picnic lunch.

From Eurong Beach Resort, continue your journey out onto Seventy-Five Mile Beach, to head 30km (19 miles) north to Eli Creek.

As the name suggests, **Seventy-Five Mile Beach** is a 120km (75-mile) stretch of uninterrupted sand, also known as the Eastern Beach, running up the eastern side of the island and flanked by dunes and rolling ocean. While driving, be alert to ocean surges, soft sand, and freshwater springs that run out from the dunes to the ocean, sometimes causing small washouts. Standard road rules apply when driving on the beach, including keeping to the left of oncoming vehicles. Small aircraft also use Seventy-Five Mile Beach as a landing strip. Aeroplanes need to land on the harder sand found close to the water's edge, so vehicles should move to the upper beach nearer the high tide line.

Millions of litres of fresh water pour out of **Eli Creek** ❺ every hour, and visitors love to swim and float down the clear-flowing stream. For an elevated view of the creek, walk the 400m/yd **Eli Creek Boardwalk**; it takes about 15 minutes.

Keep driving for 5km (3 miles) to reach the rusting relic of the **Maheno**, a

Indian Head boardwalk

trans-Tasman passenger liner that ran aground in a cyclone in 1935.

Indian Head

From the *Maheno*, continue 25km (15 miles) north along the beach to Indian Head. On the way, look for the colourful sand cliffs lining the shore near the stretch called Cathedral Beach. One section, called **The Pinnacles**, has a stunning display of yellows, browns, reds and oranges, sculpted by nature. On arrival at **Indian Head** ❻, climb to the top of this headland and you might spot whales, sharks, rays, turtles and large schools of fish in the waters below.

From Indian Head it is a 3km (2-mile) drive north to the **Champagne Pools**. These saltwater rockpools are especially beautiful at low tide, while at high tide waves crash over the rocks creating 'champagne bubbles' – a natural jacuzzi.

RETURN JOURNEY

The return journey back down the beach to Eurong is 63km (38 miles), but look out for a more direct sand track approximately 6km (3.5 miles) before you get to Eurong. Known as Cornwells Break Road, you can follow it from Seventy-Five Mile Beach for 15km (9 miles) back to **Kingfisher Bay Resort**. Grab dinner in the signature **Seabelle Restaurant** (see page 117).

LAKE WABBY

Lake Wabby ❼ is another of the island's stunning lakes, perfect for a morning swim on your third day. Set out early from the resort and turn left onto the Cornwells Break Road. After 13km (8 miles), turn right for Lake Wabby (the drive takes at least an hour). Park the car and walk the 15-minute trail to the lake, where you will be met by a desert of shifting sands called the **Stonetool Sand Blow** and the deep, emerald waters of Lake Wabby.

Leave enough time for your return journey to Kingfisher Bay Resort, and catch the return 2pm ferry back to River Heads to make it back to Brisbane by early evening.

Food and Drink

❶ MAHENO RESTAURANT

Kingfisher Bay Resort, Fraser Island; tel: 4194 9300; www.kingfisherbay.com; daily 6.30am–9pm; $$–$$$

Maheno operates with a 'paddock to plate' approach, which means that where possible the produce is sourced locally. Dinner is buffet-style, offering a selection of hot and cold dishes including local fish, king prawns and their renowned mornay of Hervey Bay scallops.

❷ MCKENZIE'S RESTAURANT

Eurong Beach Resort; tel: 4120 1600; www.eurong.com; daily 6.30am–8pm; $$
This casual restaurant with attached bar serves a buffet lunch (11.30am–2pm) of soup, salad and hot dishes, and overlooks an inviting free-form swimming pool.

White sands and crystal-clear waters

WHITSUNDAY ISLANDS

On this five-day camping and kayaking route you have the opportunity to connect with the 'other' Whitsundays. Away from the tourist crowds and luxury resorts, you will be following Aboriginal migration routes, sleeping under the stars and exploring lonely beaches on a self-propelled paddling adventure.

DISTANCE: Varies
TIME: Five days
START/END: Airlie Beach
POINTS TO NOTE: Airlie Beach, gateway to the Whitsundays, is served by the long-distance buses that ply the East Coast. You can also fly straight into the islands via Hamilton Island Airport, which has regular flights to/from both Cairns and Brisbane. Tents and cooking utensils can be hired and drinking water and food bought at Airlie Beach. A reasonable level of fitness is required for this route, along with sturdy footwear, hat, sunscreen, and insect repellent. The ideal months for camping are from May to December.

The **Whitsunday Islands** form one of the world's most beautiful archipelagos. Hundreds of secluded bays, coves and deserted beaches are dotted throughout this calm corner of the Coral Sea, which is sheltered by the Great Barrier Reef. For thousands of years, the Ngaro people lived throughout this area, leaving behind rock art, fish traps, stone tools and middens. By following part of the Ngaro Sea Trail, you will paddle in their wake while experiencing the region's natural splendour.

This is not the usual way to experience the Whitsundays; you will not be visiting lavish resorts or cruising on luxury vessels. You will be self-sufficient, but your rewards will be lonely white-sand beaches, encounters with ancient rock art and deliciously uncrowded spots for snorkelling and swimming.

AIRLIE BEACH

Airlie Beach ❶ is the hub of the Whitsunday coast and your base for exploring the islands. It is a tourist town through and through, with accommodation options for all budgets (see page 107) and a vibrant dining scene. Numerous travel agencies, posing as information centres, will vie for your patronage with sailing, diving, cruising options and more.

You can stock up on camping provisions here and, to enjoy that last restaurant meal before going camping, head to **Anchor Bar**, see ❶.

Shute Harbour

Shute Harbour ❷ is 10km (6 miles) east of Airlie Beach and is the home port for many of the vessels that service the resorts and islands. Whitsunday Island Camping Connections' 10-metre (30ft) barge, *Scamper*, designed to run up the beach to drop off campers and their gear, operates from here (book your passage: tel: 4946 6285; www.whitsundaycamp ing.com.au; fares include drinking water and use of snorkelling gear; camping equipment available to hire). The *Scamper* is generally in service all year round,

except for occasional maintenance and the wet season (usually Feb–Mar). Book campsites and buy camping permits from Queensland Parks and Wildlife Service (tel: 131304; http://parks.nprsr.qld.gov. au). Departure times from Shute Harbour are determined by the tides and there is usually one departure per day.

SOUTH MOLLE ISLAND

It takes just 15 minutes to transfer to the campsite at **Sandy Bay** ❸, on the south-western corner of **South Molle Island**.

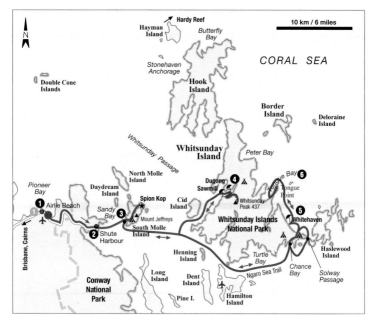

The view from Hill Inlet

Following the devastation of Cyclone Debbie, where there was once a bustling resort, there are now only ruins. Camping and bushwalking are still available, but it will be some time before the comforts of a proper resort are available again.

But with 420ha (1,000 acres) of National Park, the island still offers superb bushwalking. The walking tracks from Sandy Bay campsite to **Mount Jeffreys** and **Spion Kop** may be moderately challenging because of their length – the 11km (6.5-mile) return trip takes five hours – but you are rewarded with spectacular views. South Molle has a fascinating history of indigenous occupation, European settlement, grazing and tourism and the walk to Spion Kop passes an old Ngaro quarry, where the hillside is scattered with broken pieces of rock that were used to sharpen stone tools.

WHITSUNDAY ISLAND

The *Scamper* will return the next day (the time is dependent on tides) and take you on the 35-minute transfer to **Dugong Beach ❹**, your first camp on **Whitsunday Island**. From the beach, take the walking track to **Sawmill Beach** that leads on to **Whitsunday Peak**. This track may be one of the most challenging on the tour, reaching an elevation of 437m (1,400ft). It is a 5km (3-mile) return hike, and you should allow four hours total, to enjoy the views over the islands, turquoise waters and mainland. Steep, rocky hillsides support vine forest and open eucalypt forests, changing to grassland as you ascend. The unusual grass trees were once a source of food and tool material to the Ngaro, producing glue, fire sticks and spear handles, and yielding starch, nectar and grubs. If you are lucky you will spot white-bellied sea eagles and brahminy kites (red-backed sea eagles) soaring overhead. From May to Septem-

Whitsunday resorts

Camping is not for everyone, and although just a handful of the 74 Whitsunday Islands are home to holiday resorts, these islands are the focus of most of the Whitsunday hype. Resorts range from the super-luxurious Hayman Island by Intercontinental (www.hayman.com.au), completely renovated following Cyclone Debbie, to the more backpacker-friendly Backpackers By The Bay (www.backpackersbythebay.com). Between these extremes lies the intimate luxury of Palm Bay Resort (http://www.palmbayresort.com.au) on Long Island, the family friendly resorts of Daydream Island (www.daydreamisland.com) and Lindeman Island (www.lindeman-island-whitsundays.com.au), and the large and popular Hamilton Island (www.hamiltonisland.com.au). Many of these can be visited as a day guest from Airlie Beach or Shute Harbour, with connections operated by Cruise Whitsundays (www.cruisewhitsundays.com) and their more backpacker-orientated subsidiary Awesome Whitsundays (www.awesomewhitsundays.com).

Airlie Beach marina

ber, watch for the blows and splashes of humpback whales that use these warm waters as a calving ground.

Whitehaven Beach

Be ready for your 45-minute *Scamper* transfer to **Whitehaven Beach ❺** on the opposite side of Whitsunday Island. Ask Whitsunday Island Camping Connections to drop off kayaks (charge) for you to explore the coastline further. Brilliant white silica sand stretching for over 7km (4 miles) greets you on impossibly perfect Whitehaven Beach. The beauty of camping overnight here is that you get to experience this paradise without the crowds. While the day-trippers are basking on the sand, take the opportunity to follow the **Solway Circuit**, a 40-minute return walk, or continue on the **Chance Bay** walk, which is 7km (4 miles) long (there and back) and takes around four hours. During this walk you will pass through beach scrub and grass-tree groves to cool cedar forests, and be rewarded with stunning views over Solway Passage to Haslewood Island and south to Hamilton and Pentecost islands.

Kayak to Tongue Bay

On the afternoon of the fourth day, take to the water in your kayak and listen for the exhalations of turtles (six of the world's seven marine species are found in the Whitsundays' waters) as you paddle 6km (4 miles) north to **Tongue Bay ❻**. Here you can tackle the **Tongue Point** walk, 3km (2 miles), which takes two hours return, to drink in breathtaking views of Whitehaven Beach from **Hill Inlet lookout**. As you paddle back to Whitehaven Beach camp, explore the rich mangrove forests that flourish along the shoreline.

RETURN TO AIRLIE BEACH

On the morning of the fifth day, catch the one-hour *Scamper* transfer back to Shute Harbour and then reward your Robinson Crusoe efforts with dinner at **Mangrove Jack's** (see page 117) in Airlie Beach. Alternatively, you may want to take your adventure in a new direction: The Whitsundays are a great place to learn to sail, charter or skipper your own boat (see page 25). Scuba-diving is very popular here too (see page 29), with pristine coral reefs teeming with colourful marine life. Check out www.tourismwhitsundays.com.au for a taste of what else is on offer.

Food and Drink

❶ ANCHOR BAR

5 Golden Orchid Drive, Airlie Beach; tel: 4946 6678; www.anchorbar.com.au; daily 11am–late; $$$

This relaxed restaurant and bar overlooks Airlie Beach. From three cheese and mushroom *arancini* to start to fish tacos, it offers a variety of delicious meals. If you can't decide you can always spring for the Anchor Tasting Platter. Stay for the live local musicians or a variety of travelling acts.

Cairns seafront

CAIRNS

Cairns is a tropical outpost blessed with myriad natural charms and with more than a hint of colonial character. Set off on this leisurely stroll to capture some of the South Pacific magic that is too easily missed by those who rush straight to the reef.

DISTANCE: 6.5km (4 miles), not including Red Arrow Circuit
TIME: A half-day
START: Marlin Marina
END: Botanic Gardens
POINTS TO NOTE: Cairns Airport has regular flights direct from most state capitals, and long-distance buses connect Cairns with Brisbane and all major stops in between. Queensland Rail (www.queenslandrailtravel.com. au) runs a service five times a week between Brisbane and Cairns.

Cairns preserves much of its early beginnings as a port for inland goldfields and a centre for sugar-cane production, with several examples of tropical colonial architecture. Other industries have succeeded here, but none more so than the Great Barrier Reef tourism that powers the town today. Cairns is at its busiest in the southern states' winter holidays, when Melbournians and Sydneysiders come flocking in their thousands to escape the chill.

When Captain James Cook sailed past in 1770, gingerly negotiating the same offshore coral reefs that now pull in thousands of his fellow curious countrymen (and women), the hills and coastal flats around present-day Cairns were the home to several tribes of the Djabugay language group, including the Yidinji people. Today, local indigenous culture is vibrant and celebrated throughout the region.

MARLIN MARINA

Start at **Marlin Marina ❶**, the berth for the massive wave-piercing catamarans that whisk people to the coral reefs every day. At the **Reef Fleet Terminal** the major cruise operators are represented, making this a good place to peruse what is on offer. Lunch here at **Boatshed**, while watching the comings and goings of the waterfront, see ❶.

A boardwalk hugs the Trinity Inlet shoreline fronting the marina. The two major jetties that embrace the marina are open to all, though it is prohibited to enter the smaller jetties where private craft are moored. Take a look at what the

Cairns Regional Gallery

fishermen are catching as you wander north along the boardwalk with the boats on your right. To the left, the upmarket Shangri-La Hotel occupies the upper floors of **The Pier** complex. An elevated veranda skirts the complex and is home to numerous restaurants and bars. Continue on to **Marina Point**, the location of the **Cairns Yacht Club** and the very popular **Salt House** (see page 118), a huge

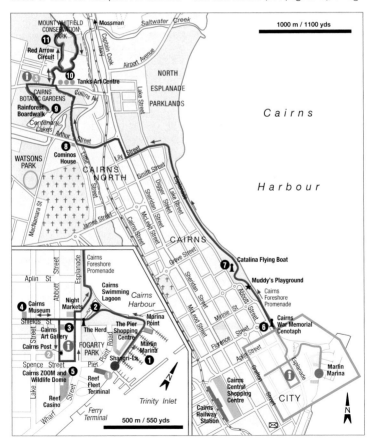

Cairns Swimming Lagoon

The exterior of Cairns Regional Gallery

outdoor restaurant and bar, offering panoramas of the harbour, city and the blue-green hills of Yarrabah.

CAIRNS SWIMMING LAGOON

When you reach the Cairns Harbour wall, turn left and follow the sweeping path along the shore. At high tide, the water laps the narrow sandy beach and when it recedes, Cairns' famous mudflats are exposed. The mud is a feeding platter for hundreds of water birds, some of which migrate from as far away as Siberia, and even the occasional crocodile (keep your eyes peeled).

Cairns is blessed with year-round warm temperatures, ranging from 25–33°C (77–91°F), but in summer, humidity often gets extremely high, and it can be huge relief to spy a metal fish spraying water, a sight that heralds the **Cairns Swimming Lagoon** ❷ (Thur–Tue 6am–10pm, Wed noon–9pm, free). Swimming in the stinger-free clear waters of this vast saltwater pool and lying around on the manicured lawns is virtually mandatory for all visitors, and you might also want to check out *The Herd*, a delightful granite sculpture at the tail end of the lagoon.

CULTURAL CAIRNS

Cross the **Esplanade** here and head along Shields Street to the **Cairns Art Gallery** ❸ (corner of Shields and Abbott streets; www.cairnsregionalgallery. au; Mon–Fri 9am–5pm, Sat 10am–5pm, Sun 10am–2pm; charge). Exhibits include the gallery's collection of international and Australian artists – with a particular focus on indigenous artists and those from the tropical north – plus visiting exhibitions.

Walk westwards on Shields Street to the intersection with Lake Street where the **Cairns Museum** ❹ (corner Shields and Lake streets; Mon–Sat 10am–4pm; charge) occupies the balconied former School of Arts building and showcases a fascinating collection of items from the Cairns Historical Society.

Make your way back along Shields Street and turn right on Abbott Street. On the left-hand side of the street you pass several heritage buildings converted to a variety of modern uses: the **Courthouse Hotel** was once the Cairns courthouse, but occupying its 1882 building, the **Cairns Post** still produces the local newspapers. Turn left at Spence Street to head back to the Esplanade, but not before grabbing a quality cup of coffee at **Bang and Grind**, see ❷.

CAIRNS WILDLIFE DOME

On the right is the **Reef Casino**, the top floor of which houses the **Cairns ZOOM and Wildlife Dome** ❺ (www.cairnszoom. com.au; daily 9am–6.15pm; charge). You can choose from a number of different climbs that cater to all ages, experiences and fitness levels – from the hardcore Commando Rope Climb to the less challenging Mid-Zoom. The Dome-Climb

"Goliath", Cairns Wildlife Dome

allows you to see Cairns from every conceivable angle. Set aside about an hour to explore, but remember your ticket is valid for five days so you can return any time.

NIGHT MARKETS

Cross over Shields Street, to the **Night Markets** (daily 4.30pm–11pm), a raggedy collection of food and merchandise stalls that swings into life at dusk. Cross the Esplanade, skirt the northwestern shore of the Lagoon and join the **Cairns Foreshore Promenade**.

CAIRNS FORESHORE PROMENADE

The promenade hugs the shoreline almost as far as the airport. During the day, shade is available, but scarce, so be prepared and carry plenty of drinking water. Information panels along the walk describe the history and ecology of the Cairns region. Two artillery pieces flank the **Cairns War Memorial Cenotaph** ❻, erected to commemorate those from Cairns who died in World War I. The clock faces are painted permanently showing 4.28am, the time at which the ANZAC landing at Gallipoli began on 25 April 1915.

Continue along the promenade, through **Muddy's Playground** (daily 7am–8pm), a wet and wild playground for little kids with a welcome café where you can grab a cool drink.

Nearby, atop a tall plinth, is a tiny commemorative model of a **Catalina flying boat** ❼, a one-time frequent visitor to Trinity Inlet during World War II. From their base at Cairns, these remarkable aircraft flew patrols of up to 24 hours in duration, locating and attacking ships of the Japanese fleet.

Pass behind the children's playground pirate ship as the path swings inland and continue north along the Esplanade as it sweeps around to the left and turns into Lily Street. Continue down Lily Street, cross busy Sheridan Street at the lights and turn right, walking one block down Sheridan. Turn left into Arthur Street (which becomes Greenslopes Street), and then go over the railway crossing and Lily Creek bridge.

On the next corner is **Cominos House** ❽ (Mon–Fri 9.30am–4pm), a colonial-style home on stilts that was the residence of one of Cairns's earliest settler families until 1988. Relocated from its original Abbott Street site, it has been adapted into an environmental and arts centre.

BOTANIC GARDENS

Opposite and on your right is a path leading into the **Cairns Botanic Gardens** ❾ (daily 7.30am–5.30pm; free). Enter the shady gardens and cross the narrow footbridge over the mangrove-lined Saltwater Creek. Just after the crossing, take the right fork on the path and then the left fork a little further on. The dense bush on your left closely represents the rainforest before

Cairns Botanic Gardens

Monument to the RAAF

European settlement, with huge swamp paperbarks and other native trees (many of them labelled).

You'll soon emerge onto Collins Avenue opposite the **Tanks Art Centre** ❿ (www.tanksartscentre.com; Mon–Fri 8.30am–4.30pm; free gallery entry), an extraordinary contemporary art and performance facility creatively housed in three massive World War II oil-storage tanks. These three tanks were completed for the Royal Australian Navy in 1944 and camouflaged here to store crude oil for the war effort. In the early 1990s, talk of removing the tanks caused a massive outcry, so it was decided to redevelop the site into this unique and heritage-listed arts space.

If you have the energy, continue up the hill past the tanks to the **Mount Whitfield Conservation Park** ⓫ and the **Red Arrow Circuit** (1.5km/1 mile). There are some steep sections to this track, but the rewards include walking through virgin rainforest and sweeping views over Cairns and Trinity Bay.

Walking west on Collins Avenue, you soon reach the original Botanic Gardens entrance and the information centre, toilets, orchid house and **Botanic Gardens Restaurant and Cafe**, which is the perfect place for lunch, see ❸. Afterwards you can walk it off on the **Rainforest Boardwalk**, starting opposite the main entrance and winding through lush tropical rainforest.

From here, the best way to return is to catch a bus on Collins Avenue. There is a stop right outside the original entrance. Or wander back through the gardens and catch a bus from Sheridan Street. Otherwise, call a taxi (tel: 131008 for Black & White taxis).

Food and Drink

❶ BOATSHED

1 Cairns Harbour Lights, 8/1 Marlin Parade; tel: 4031 4748; http://www.boatshedcairns.com.au; daily 11.30am–9.30pm; $$–$$$

At the wharf end of the Reef Fleet Terminal, the Boatshed serves a wide range of seafood, indulgent desserts and even 'dessert cocktails'. On Sundays they lay on '$1 oysters' and live music.

❷ BANG AND GRIND

8/14 Spence St, tel 4051 7770; Mon–Fri 6am–3pm, Sat 6.30am–2.30pm, Sun 7.30am–12.30pm; $

One of Far North Queensland's craft coffee outlets that is delighting latte loving hipsters from further south (and anyone else who appreciates a good cup of caffeine).

❸ BOTANIC GARDENS RESTAURANT AND CAFE

Collins Avenue; tel: 4053 7087; www.cafebotanic.com.au; daily 7am–4.30pm; $

Enjoy a light salad, or maybe one of the sinfully sticky waffles, under a canopy of tropical rainforest trees.

Soaring over the rainforest on the Skyrail Cableway

KURANDA CIRCUIT

Silently glide over a green sea of trees on the award–winning Skyrail Rainforest Cableway to pretty Kuranda, situated on the lush highlands above Cairns. Kuranda is encircled by rainforest and renowned for arts, crafts and its alternative lifestyle.

DISTANCE: 44.5km (27 miles) of which 3km (2 miles) is on foot
TIME: A full day
START: Caravonica Terminal
END: Freshwater Railway Station
POINTS TO NOTE: Book ahead through your accommodation or directly with Skyrail (www.skyrail.com.au) or Kuranda Scenic Railway (www.ksr.com.au). Both offer railway/cableway packages. You can also get bus transfers from your accommodation to either terminal and from one terminal to the other (handy if you self-drive). Book your departure time for 9am; the last train leaves Kuranda at 3.30pm. This tour can also be done by ascending on the railway and returning on the cableway, or just doing a round trip on either the cableway or railway. Check out available packages, which allow you to bundle your Skyrail booking with entry to some of Kuranda's attractions.

Your journey on the **Skyrail Rainforest Cableway** launches from **Caravon-ica Terminal ❶** in Smithfield (corner of Cairns Western Arterial Road and Captain Cook Highway), a 15-minute drive north of Cairns along the Captain Cook Highway. The 7.5km (4.5-mile) aerial journey takes approximately 1.5 hours, including two informative stops along the way where you can get out and explore the rainforest of **Barron Gorge National Park**.

SKYRAIL RAINFOREST RAILWAY

As you set off from Caravonica Terminal and skim above the **MacAlister Range**, the dense canopy of World Heritage tropical rainforest – the most ancient 'old-growth' tropical rainforest on Earth and home to an amazing diversity of life – stretches out below. The rainforest actually extends over 500km (300 miles) along the north Queensland coastline. Look back for a spectacular view of Cairns out to the Coral Sea. At the first stop, at **Red Peak ❷**, you can join the complimentary ranger-guided walks along a short boardwalk surrounded by giant ferns, lush palms and towering trees. Together with interpretive signs,

Barron Gorge

the rangers will help you identify some of the rainforest's more interesting and unusual species. Re-board a gondola for the short journey to the second stop.

Barron Falls

At **Barron Falls** ❸ you disembark onto a boardwalk that leads to three lookouts providing breathtaking forest-framed views of the mighty gorge and falls. Especially impressive when the Barron is in full flood during the wet season (Dec–Mar), the flow drastically reduces for the rest of the year (so do not be put off if your visit coincides with some rain, as this is when the rainforest is at its very best, shrouded in mist and streaked with thundering waterfalls). Here you will find the **Rainforest Interpretation Centre**, with interactive displays, videos, and information that will help unravel some of the mysteries of this fascinating ecosystem. Re-board a gondola for the final 10-minute journey over the rainforest and the impressive **Barron River** to Kuranda village.

KURANDA

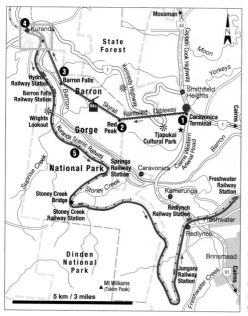

Skyrail's Kuranda terminal is adjacent to the **Kuranda Railway Station**, from where it is just a short wander along Coondoo Street to heart of gorgeous **Kuranda village** ❹. It is exceedingly easy to lose several hours leisurely strolling among the shops, cafés and wildlife attractions including the Kuranda Koala Gardens and Australian Butterfly Sanctuary. Discovered in the 1960s by hippies who wanted to live an alternative lifestyle in idyllic surroundings, the rainforest village continues to attract legions of talented artists and craftspeople today, hence the plethora of bustling markets.

The Kuranda Scenic Railway

There are plenty of places for a break, such as the **Petit Café** , see ➊, on Therwine Street. Where Therwine intersects with Coondoo Street you will see **Centenary Park**, home to the very helpful **Kuranda Visitor Information Centre** (www.kuranda.org; daily 10am–4pm). From here you can start on an easy, one-hour, 3km (2-mile) circuit walk that combines the Jumrum Creek, Jungle Walk and River Walk trails.

Markets

Turn right turn from Coondoo Street and head along Therwine Street. On the right are the **Kuranda Original Rainforest Markets** Ⓐ (corner Therwine and Thooree streets; www.kurandaoriginalrainforestmarket.com.au; daily 9.30am–3pm), a village within a village, with locally-made fashions, crafts and foods. Diagonally across the road are the **Heritage Markets** (Rob Veivers Drive; www.kurandamarkets.com; daily 9.30am–3.30pm),

with yet more souvenirs. Enjoy lunch at one of Kuranda's oldest establishments, **Frogs Restaurant**, see ➋. The market areas overflow with crafts and produce. The rainforest surrounding Kuranda has been home to the Djabugay people for over 10,000 years, making it a popular spot to pick up a didgeridoo.

Kuranda attractions

At the rear of the Heritage Markets is **BirdWorld Kuranda** Ⓑ (www.birdworldkuranda.com; daily 9am–4pm; charge), home to the largest single collection of free-flying birds in Australia. Nearly 60 species of the most spectacular birds from all corners of the planet are on display here, including Australia's endangered, flightless giant – the cassowary.

A walkway links BirdWorld to two more wildlife attractions. The **Australian Butterfly Sanctuary** Ⓒ (8 Rob Veivers Drive; www.australianbutterflies.com; daily 9.45am–4pm; charge) is the largest butterfly enclosure in Australia. The flight aviary is home to over 2,000 tropical butterflies, including the spectacular Cairns birdwing. On the other side of BirdWorld is **Kuranda Koala Gardens** Ⓓ (www.koalagardens.com; daily 9am–4pm; charge), where you can get your photo taken cuddling a koala (though it is important to consider that koa-

las can become stressed by this kind of human interaction – observing them can be just as rewarding), watch wombats and kangaroos, spot a freshwater crocodile and brave the walk-through snake house.

Just down the road, **BatReach** (Jungle Walk, Coondoo Street; www.batreach. com/home.html; Tue–Fri and Sun 10.30am–2.30pm; admission by donation) is a rescue and rehabilitation centre for flying foxes and micro bats.

Back on Coondoo Street recharge at **Kuranda Coffee Republic**, see ③.

KURANDA SCENIC RAILWAY

Make your way back to Kuranda Railway Station for the 3.30pm departure of the **Kuranda Scenic Railway** ❺, a 90-minute journey through deep ravines and lush rainforest and past spectacular waterfalls. Constructed between 1882 and 1891, the railway is a tremendous feat of engineering. Hundreds of men were employed to build the 15 hand-dug tunnels and 37 bridges, and at least 23 workers died before the railway opened up the rich Atherton Tablelands.

There is a brief photo stop at the station overlooking **Barron Falls** to see the river plunge (or trickle, depending on the time of year) from its placid Kuranda reaches into the gorge. The train also slows over a picturesque gully as it crosses **Stoney Creek Bridge**, with a backdrop of one of the region's most spectacular waterfalls. Eventually you will arrive at newly refurbished **Freshwater Railway Station** to catch your transfer bus back to Cairns or the Skyrail terminal.

Food and Drink

① PETIT CAFÉ

Kuranda Original Rainforest Markets, Shop 19, Therwine St; tel: 421 799 131; www. kuranda.org/listing/petit-cafe-kuranda; daily 8am–3pm; $

Located in the bustling surroundings of the Rainforest Markets, this charming café serves authentic freshly-made French crepes – both savoury and sweet – as well as French cider and locally-grown biodynamic coffee.

② FROGS RESTAURANT

2/4 Rob Veivers Drive; tel: 4093 8952; www. frogsrestaurant.com.au; daily 9am–3.30pm; $$

Built in 1923, and one of Kuranda's first cafés, this licensed restaurant has recently relocated to the Heritage Markets, where you can sit on the verandah with superb rainforest views and enjoy an extensive menu ranging from gourmet pizzas to fresh local barramundi.

③ KURANDA COFFEE REPUBLIC

24 Coondoo Street; tel: 459 233 274; Mon–Sat 6am–3pm, Sun 7am–3pm; $

Locally grown beans and unique blends are the reasons to visit this café. You may end up leaving with a large bag of coffee beans for yourself.

PORT DOUGLAS AND MOSSMAN GORGE

Travel north from Cairns along one of Australia's most spectacular coastal roads with dramatic views of the Coral Sea. Discover the seaside towns of Port Douglas and Palm Cove, and float in the crystal-clear waters of Mossman Gorge.

DISTANCE: 182km (110 miles)
TIME: A full day
START/END: Cairns
POINTS TO NOTE: You will need a car for this trip, and don't forget your swimming gear. This tour can be combined with Route 13; Daintree village is a 35km (21-mile) drive north of Mossman.

This journey past Cairns' northern beaches unveils golden swathes of palm-fringed sand along a 26km (16-mile) stretch of unspoilt tropical shoreline, fronted by the Coral Sea and backed by rainforest-clad mountains. Small, laid-back villages, mixing residential with low-key tourism development, rest lazily beside the sea. Further on, the larger, glitzier towns of Palm Cove and Port Douglas lure an eclectic crowd of backpackers, blingy botoxed retirees and a few well-heeled international visitors.

TO PORT DOUGLAS

Make an early start from Cairns and head north on the Captain Cook High-way for 67km (40 miles) to Port Douglas. As you leave Cairns you will pass the **Skyrail Rainforest Cableway** (see page 78) to Kuranda and **Tjapukai Cultural Park** (www.tjapukai.com.au; daily 9am–4.30pm, evening show 7–9.30pm; charge) a place that's ensuring a 40,000-year-old culture remains alive and which leads visitors through a dreamtime journey of creation with traditional dance, music and legends. Branching off the highway to the east are roads leading to serene beachside villages such as **Yorkeys Knob, Trinity Beach, Palm Cove** and **Ellis Beach**. Just after **Palm Cove** (see page 85), and Wangetti Beach, be sure to pause at **Rex Lookout** to take in the panoramic views across Trinity Bay. This is also a popular launch spot for hang gliders and gets busy at weekends.

Wildlife Habitat

Just before the entrance to Port Douglas is the **Wildlife Habitat ❶** (Corner Captain Cook Highway and Port Douglas Road; www.wildlifehabitat.com.au; daily 8am–5pm; charge), where you can

Looking over Port Douglas

experience **Breakfast with the Birds**, see ①, and then enjoy presentations on the local ecology of wetlands, rainforest and grasslands.

PORT DOUGLAS

From here it is only 6km (3.5 miles) to the heart of **Port Douglas ❷** (or Port, as it's known to the locals). Not very long ago, Port Douglas was a sleepy seaside settlement. Today, it has been transformed into a fashionable tropical holiday resort, with the whole spectrum of tourist accommodation, award-winning restaurants, beautiful galleries and upmarket shopping. Fortunately, the transition has not entirely robbed Port Douglas of its natural charm.

The approach from the main road is lined by an avenue of about 450 huge African oil palms; as many again are planted around the **Sheraton Mirage Resort** and the **Marina Mirage**. They form part of the extravagant vision of former multi-millionaire Christopher Skase, who transplanted the trees here at a cost of about A$1,500 each. Skase went spectacularly bust in a series of media and leisure ventures in the late 1980s; happily, Port Douglas fared better and has continued to prosper.

Macrossan Street

The main drag, **Macrossan Street**, is lined with a colourful array of shops, eateries and restaurants, and is well worth a wander. The sidewalks are thronged with casual pedestrians, who seem to have all the time (and money)

in the world. With a core population of approximately 4,000 people, the town also sports a world-class marina and international-standard golf courses.

At the western end of Macrossan Street (on the corner with Wharf Street), the Court House Hotel is the oldest pub in town (in operation since 1878) . Across the road is **Anzac Park**, which overflows with market

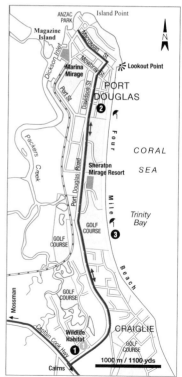

Lounging on Palm Cove's beach

stalls on Sunday mornings (8am–2pm), selling arts and crafts as well as fresh fruit and vegetables.

Four Mile Beach

Along the southeastern side of the peninsula, **Four Mile Beach** ❸ is the town's prime asset: a long, lonely stretch of sand, with no signs of development (accommodation and houses are hidden behind the palms). Swimming is reasonably safe (there are life guards), but stay inside the stinger nets during stinger season (Oct–May, see page 28).

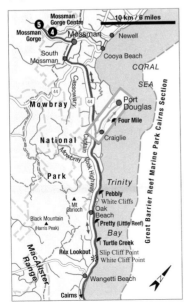

TO MOSSMAN GORGE

Take the main road out of Port Douglas back to the Captain Cook Highway. Turn right for the 26km (16-mile) drive north to Mossman. Turn left at Mossman and follow the signs for 5km (3 miles) to Mossman Gorge.

On the way to the gorge is the **Mossman Gorge Centre** ❹ (www.mossman gorge.com.au/the-centre/the-centre; daily 8am–6pm. The Kuku Yalanji are the indigenous inhabitants of this land, which stretches from around Cooktown in the north to near Chillagoe in the west and Port Douglas in the south. The centre's Aboriginal Art Gallery is well worth a browse. They also offer 90-minute guided walks (charge) around Mossman Gorge, visiting culturally significant sites, sharing dreamtime legends and providing an insight into their traditional relationship with this unique tropical environment.

MOSSMAN GORGE

Make your way to the car park for spectacular **Mossman Gorge** ❺. In the **Mossman River** swimming is generally safe and crocodile-free but always exercise caution. The short **River Circuit track** (10 minutes) takes you to a viewing platform over the river, but if you would like to go on a longer walk and escape the crowds, take the 3km (2-mile) **Rainforest Circuit track** (approximately one hour return). For a really different experience, check out the River Snorkelling

In Mossman Gorge   *A furry face at Cairns Tropical Zoo*

tours offered by local operators Back Country Bliss (www.backcountrybliss. com.au). These tours involve a three-hour swim along the Mossman River, through the Daintree Rainforest, as your guide explains the symbiotic relationship between the rainforest and the reef. Be warned – most other rivers around here are not croc free, so don't try and do this on your own.

PALM COVE

Head back along the Captain Cook High-way towards Cairns. After about 50km (30

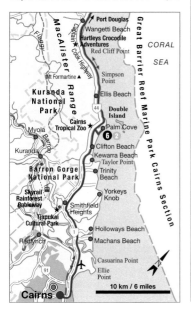

miles) turn left for **Palm Cove** ❻, a beach-side development (some might say over-development) where the brick-cobbled streets and 500-year-old melaleuca trees bestow a wonderfully tranquil mood. With its exclusive hotels and resorts, restaurants and spas, this spot is about sheer relaxation, pampering and fine-dining. For a casual evening meal or drink overlooking the sea, try **Il Forno**, see ❷. From here it is a 30-minute drive back to Cairns on the Captain Cook Highway.

Food and Drink

❶ BREAKFAST WITH THE BIRDS

Wildlife Habitat, corner Captain Cook Highway and Port Douglas Road; tel: 4099 3235; www.wildlifehabitat.com.au; daily 9–10.30am; $$$

Enjoy a full buffet breakfast with fruits, pastries, cereals and hot food from the BBQ while immersing yourself in the wetlands environment and being joined by a throng of birds that wander freely amid the tables.

❷ IL FORNO

7/111-117 Williams Esplanade, Palm Cove; tel: 4059 1666; www. ilfornopalmcove.com; daily 5.30pm-9.30pm; $$

In a divine setting, with a great outlook over the Coral Sea, Il Forno is all about relaxed dining. Enjoy a cool drink, savour one of their traditional Roman-style pizzas and follow up with one of their delicious desserts.

Daintree River from above

DAINTREE AND CAPE TRIBULATION

Take a full day to drive through the spectacular Wet Tropics and Daintree Unesco World Heritage site. Spot crocs on the river, wander boardwalks through mangroves, take a dip at Mason's swimming hole and enjoy sweeping, deserted beaches.

DISTANCE: 44km (26 miles)
TIME: A full day
START: Daintree
END: Cape Tribulation
POINTS TO NOTE: Daintree is 110km (66 miles) north of Cairns via Mossman; alternatively, this route could easily be linked with Route 12. A car is needed for this route and you will need to bring cash to pay for the ferry across the river. Consider overnighting in the rainforest to maximise your wilderness experience with adventures such as nocturnal wildlife walks and jungle surfing through the canopy. Book your morning Daintree River cruise in advance.

The Daintree River, one of the longest rivers on Australia's East Coast, was named by George Elphinstone Dalrymple after his friend Richard Daintree, an English geologist. Dalrymple wrote 'No river in North Australia possesses surroundings combining so much of distant mountain grandeur with local beauty and wealth of vegetation'.

DAINTREE

Daintree ❶ is a tiny, historic village on the southern bank of the scenic Daintree River overlooked by Queensland's third-highest mountain, **Thornton Peak** (1,374m/4,508ft). It's a picturesque setting, originally the base for 'cedar-getters' who came to log prized red cedar, which once flourished in the area. There's not much more here to detain you other than the **Daintree Village General Store and Restaurant**, see ❶, which can supply you with information on the area and sell tickets for a Daintree River Cruise, if you haven't already booked.

River cruises
Daintree River cruises take place on several different sections of the river. The tours take you up or downstream, through narrow reaches lined with mangroves and rainforests that are rich in wildlife. It is unusual not to spot a crocodile from a safe distance, especially in the cooler months when the huge reptiles leave the water to sun themselves on the riverbank. The departure jetty for many of

The Daintree Ferry

the river cruises is a short downhill stroll from the Daintree Village General Store. Operators include Crocodile Express (www.crocodileexpress.com; daily one-hour cruises 8.30am–3.30pm) and Bruce Belcher's Daintree River Cruises (www.daintreerivercruises.com.au; daily one-hour cruises).

Daintree Ferry

Drive east along Daintree Road for 10km (6 miles) to the turnoff to the **Daintree Ferry ❷** (5am–midnight; charge). On the other side of the two-minute crossing, a good sealed road tunnels through overhanging trees all the way to Cape Tribulation. Take care on the narrow, winding stretches that hug the cliff edges. Speed bumps are placed along the road to slow traffic in areas where southern cassowaries – large, flightless birds that can be very aggressive towards humans – may be encountered. Cassowaries undertake a key role in the rainforest, spreading tree seeds after they have digested the fruit. Sadly it is quite rare to observe these extraordinary animals in the wild, but if you do see one, it is

best to keep your distance, particularly if they are in a family group with young (and definitely don't get in between the adults and the chicks, as they are aggressively protective parents).

After 8km (5 miles) you reach the **Alexandra Range Lookout**, with sweeping views back to the south, across the wide mouth of the Daintree

Kulki track lookout

River, to Snapper Island and the sugar-cane fields and ranges beyond.

Daintree Discovery Centre

A little further north, pull over at the **Daintree Discovery Centre** ❸ (www.daintree-rec.com.au; daily 8.30am–5pm; charge). This award-wining interpretive centre provides a rainforest booklet and comprehensive audio guides that together give you an excellent insight into what you see as you self-guide along the low-impact boardwalk and ascend the awe-inspiring heights of the Canopy Tower. Standing 23m (76ft) tall, and featuring five viewing platforms, the tower provides a fantastic experience for photographers, botany enthusiasts and birdwatchers alike. Take some time to visit the Jurassic Forest and the models of dinosaurs that may have lived in various locations around Queensland during the Jurassic Period.

TO CAPE TRIBULATION

Drive further north, passing the **Cow Bay Hotel Motel** and then **Thornton Beach**, where you can stop for a stroll along a peaceful stretch of sand backed by dense rainforest. You can walk to the mouth of **Cooper Creek**, one of Australia's richest mangrove ecosystems (but watch out for crocodiles).

Continue north to reach the **Marrdja Boardwalk** ❹, a short (30-minute) loop walk beside a running rocky stream, through lush rainforest and mangroves. A little further north again is **Mason's Café, Store and Tours** (Cape Tribulation Road; www.masonstours.com.au), which offers guided day and night walks, 4WD tours and croc-spotting (as well as great milkshakes and food). If you want to cool down, a little path behind the store leads to **Mason's swimming hole**, a lovely spot where you can rope-swing into the cool water of Myall Creek.

CAPE TRIBULATION

It is just a short drive from Mason's Café to **Cape Tribulation** ❺. The cape was so named by Captain Cook in 1770, 'because here began all our troubles'.

Old-growth rainforest

The tropical rainforest stretching from just north of Cairns through Cape Tribulation and on to Cooktown is around 110 million years old, and a remnant of the extensive forest that used to cover most of Australia and, before that, Gondwanaland. With this extraordinary ancestry, the north Queensland rainforest boasts the highest number of endemic species in the world, and is rightfully recognised and protected within the Wet Tropics World Heritage Area. Some of the most accessible rainforest is in the Daintree National Park, showcased by the Daintree Discovery Centre.

Experiencing the rainforest from a zipline

Just after the 'Welcome to Cape Tribulation' sign, turn right into the **Dubuji Visitor Area** and walk the easy 1km (0.65-mile) boardwalk loop around freshwater swamps and mangroves, which also has access to the expansive **Myall Beach**.

Cape Tribulation consists only of a small cluster of shops, including a pharmacy, small supermarket and PK's Jungle Village, a backpackers' resort with a rowdy bar. Continue 1km (0.65 mile) north to **Kulki–Cape Tribulation Beach**, where there is an easy pathway to an elevated lookout over Cape Tribulation Beach and a rough track over the headland to Myall Beach. These two magnificent, picture-postcard beaches, where golden sands and azure waters rim the deep-green rainforest, are the main drawcard and the climax of the drive. Do not be alarmed by the harmless goannas (large monitor lizards) which hang out here scavenging from picnickers.

For the adventurous, **Jungle Surfing Canopy Tours** (Cape Tribulation; www.junglesurfing.com.au; daily 8.30am–5pm; charge) offer an exhilarating way to experience the rainforest from above, on flying-fox ziplines, stopping at five tree platforms to take in the bird's-eye views.

If you want to escape the cape and hit the coral, from the Daintree/Cape Tribulation area it is only 30–40 minutes by boat to the Great Barrier Reef. Snorkelling and diving trips are run by

Ocean Safari (www.oceansafari.com.au; morning and afternoon trips available depending on season; charge).

From here, the road north is unsealed and only accessible by 4WD. It is approximately 2.5 hours' drive south from Cape Tribulation to Cairns – if you're looking to grab a bite to eat before heading back, check out **Whet Café and Bar**, see ❷, in Cape Tribulation, a real culinary surprise in the midst of the jungle.

Food and Drink

❶ DAINTREE VILLAGE GENERAL STORE AND RESTAURANT

1 Stewart Street, Daintree; tel: 4098 6146; daily 8am–7.30pm; $$

Lunch and dinner options featuring local fauna include crocodile burgers and pan-fried locally-caught barramundi. Also on offer is a selection of freshly baked cakes and scones. BYO beer and wine can be bought at the general store.

❷ WHET CAFÉ AND BAR

Cape Tribulation Road, Cape Tribulation; tel: 4098 0007; www.whet.net.au; daily 11am–3pm, 6pm–8pm; $$

It's not easy finding fine dining this far north, but bucking this trend with sublime style are the crew behind Whet, who serve fabulous food and ensure it's accompanied with a fantastic atmosphere. Try the scallops and the barramundi.

The granite gorge in Davies Creek National Park

ATHERTON TABLELANDS

Discover the charm of the Atherton Tablelands, also known as the Cairns Highlands, on this two-day drive visiting a plateau of patchwork farms, volcanic lakes and tumbling waterfalls. On the way, sample some of the world's best coffee in Mareeba and overnight in historic Yungaburra.

DISTANCE: Day one to Yungaburra: 120km (72 miles); day two: 70km (42 miles)
TIME: Two days
START: Cairns
END: Crawford's Lookout
POINTS TO NOTE: You will need a car, and to stay overnight in Yungaburra (see page 111). For Kuranda see route 11. Instead of returning straight to Cairns at the end of the trip, you could carry on to Mission Beach, or visit some of the sights on the way to Cairns on that route (see page 96).

The Tablelands have long been known as the food bowl of the Tropics. Incorporating the townships of Mareeba, Atherton, Herberton, Ravenshoe, Millaa Millaa and Malanda, the region is renowned for its dairy products and for growing tea, coffee and sugar. Combine this bountiful larder with the invigorating natural beauty of fast-flowing waterfalls, pristine lakes and crystal streams, and you have a destination that revitalises the five senses. More recently, the region has also become known for the quality of its mountain biking, with an extensive trail network being put into the forests around several of the Tableland towns, including a particularly good one near Davies Creek near Mareeba.

TO MAREEBA

Leave Cairns early and head northwest for 13km (8 miles) on the Captain Cook Highway to the Smithfield roundabout. Take the road to Kuranda (see page 79), a 30-minute winding drive through dense rainforest, and then follow the signs along the Kennedy Highway to Mareeba where the vegetation suddenly changes from rainforest to dry bush. The change is brought about by two factors: less rainfall and different soil. This heralds the beginning of the Atherton Tablelands: rich, rolling country, much of which is cultivated for agriculture.

Davies Creek National Park
After crossing Davies Creek, take the road on the left that leads to the **Davies**

Mareeba's landscape

Creek National Park ❶. This road is unsealed for 7km (4 miles) but is driveable in a conventional vehicle. The creek winds and falls through a granite gorge, providing the opportunity for a quick dip in dozens of rocky plunge pools. Beyond the campground there is a 2km (1-mile) walk to lookouts above **Davies Creek Falls**, and a short circuit track leads to a sandy picnic area where platypus may be spotted in the adjacent creek. Visitors with their own tents will find a great overnight spot at Lower Davies Creek camping area, which is accessible in a normal car for most of the year.

Head back out onto the Kennedy Highway, where the bush soon gives way to open farmland with mango, citrus and avocado orchards.

MAREEBA

Mareeba is the centre of the country's coffee-growing region, with over 75 percent of Aus-

On the shores of Lake Barrine

tralia's crop grown in the district's fertile soils. Before you enter the town, about 5km (3 miles) from the Davies Creek turnoff, billboards direct you to **Jaques Coffee Plantation** ❷ (www. jaquescoffee.com). It is a 4km (2.5-mile) detour along Gilmore Road and well worth the effort for an insight into the coffee industry. Take a 20-minute tour (charge), followed by coffee- or liqueur-tasting, or just sample the produce at **Jaques Coffee Plantation Café**, see ❶.

Back on the highway, proceed into the town of **Mareeba**, where the **Coffee Works Experience** (136 Mason Street; www.coffeeworks.com.au) offers a coffee gift shop, coffee-tasting and a café. Tea-drinkers are also catered for!

TO ATHERTON

During World War II, the Atherton Tablelands area became a large military base, supporting between 100,000 and 300,000 troops from 140 different units, and Mareeba played a major role in the Battle of the Coral Sea. As you head south out of town on the Kennedy Highway there is an interesting historic collection, The **Warbird Adventures**, ❸ site (Mareeba Airport; www.warbirdadventures.com.au; Wed–Sun 10am–4pm) where you can view one of several ex-military aircraft including a C47 Douglas DC3 and a Winjeel. There are usually a few different on-going resto-ration projects of various other aircraft as well.

Continue your journey southwards towards **Walkamin**. Just before the town, the **Mount Uncle Distillery** (1819 Chewko Road; www.mtuncle.com; daily 10am–4pm) bottles and sells premium liqueurs and spirits distilled from tropical products such as coffee, limes and macadamia nuts. In the tiny township of Tolga, the **Tolga Bakery**, see ❷, has quite a reputation for home-style cooking including a wide variety of pies and great coffee.

ATHERTON

Just five minutes down the road from Tolga is the town of **Atherton** ❹. The **Atherton Information Centre** (corner Main Street and Silo Road; www.trc.qld.gov.au/locations/atherton-tableland-information-centre; daily 9am–5pm) provides maps and brochures and makes accommodation bookings. One of the town's attractions is the **Crystal Caves** (69 Main Street; www.crystalcaves.com.au; daily 9am–5pm; charge), where a faux cave houses a fine collection of crystals and fossils.

Curtain Fig Tree

From Atherton, follow the signs for Malanda, then take a left turn where the signpost indicates that it's 12km (7 miles) to Yungaburra. As you approach town, detour right to the **Curtain Fig Tree** ❺. Walk along the boardwalk that

Yungaburra's church

Sampling the local coffee

surrounds the tree and an interpretive display explains how this amazing natural sculpture was formed; a draped curtain of aerial roots first grew from the parasitic strangler fig, smothering the host tree, and the whole thing then fell sideways and the fig lowered its roots to the ground.

YUNGABURRA

Yungaburra ❻ is a historic village that has changed little since 1910 and boasts no fewer than 18 heritage-listed buildings. It makes a good restful overnight base, and the **Yungaburra Visitor Centre** (Cedar Street; www.yungaburra.com; daily Mon–Sat 9am–5pm, Sun 10am–4pm) can help with booking accommodation and dining options such as atmospheric **Nick's Swiss-Italian Restaurant**, see ❸. Also worth a look is the little hidden gem, the **Whistle Stop Café** (36 Cedar Street; tel: 4095 3913; daily 7.30am–3pm; $).

Crater Lakes National Park
Just to the east of town is **Lake Eacham**, a sparkling blue lake in a drowned volcanic crater fringed by lawn and surrounded by rainforest. Along with Lake Barrine, it is the main feature of **Crater Lakes National Park** ❼, and the perfect spot for an afternoon swim and sunbathe. If you would like to stretch your legs, there is an easy 3km (2-mile) circuit around the lake. This is

also a birdwatcher's paradise, with over 180 recorded species.

About 5km (3 miles) further northeast along the Gillies Highway is Lake Eacham's twin, **Lake Barrine**. The **Lake Barrine Teahouse Restaurant**, see ❹ is an ideal breakfast spot for the second day of this route. After breakfast consider joining the **Lake Barrine Rainforest Cruise** (www.lakebarrine.com.au; charge). You will be able to spend 45 minutes cruising around the volcanic crater, listening to an informative wildlife commentary and sighting pelicans and other water birds, tortoises, fish and maybe – in the cooler months – amethystine pythons, the world's third-largest snake (growing up to 8.5 metres/28ft long) sunning themselves on branches. For good birdwatching and walking, there is a 5km (3-mile) track around the lake. A short stroll away from the restaurant is a pair of giant twin kauri pines, estimated to be 1,000 years old.

MALANDA

From Lake Eacham, take the road south to **Malanda**, amid lush green pastures over red volcanic soil. The black-and-white Friesian cows grazing in these pastures each produce up to 30 litres (6.5 gallons) of milk a day. The **Malanda Dairy Centre** (8 James Street; www.malandadairycentre.com; Wed–Sun 9am–3pm; charge) runs factory tours

and serves up a seriously good milk-shake. You can also check out their on-site art gallery. If, after yesterday's focus on coffee, you are interested in finding out how tea is grown and pro-cessed, call into the **Nerada Tea Vis-itor Centre** (www.neradatea.com.au; daily 9am–4pm), just 10km (6 miles) outside of Malanda on the Glen Allyn Road. Back on the Malanda–Millaa Mil-laa Road, consider stopping at the Aus-tralian Platypus Park at Tarzali Lakes for the **Smokehouse Cafe**, see ➎.

MILLAA MILLAA AND THE WATERFALL CIRCUIT

Continue along the highway for about 15km (9 miles) through farmland and rainforest to **Millaa Millaa ➑**, another dairy town, ringed by some of the Table-lands' most spectacular waterfalls. Enter the **Waterfall Circuit** by taking the Theresa Creek Road, 1km (0.65 mile) east of Millaa Millaa on the Palm-erston Highway. The first stop is **Millaa Millaa Falls**, considered to be the per-fect 'drop' of water and used in many shampoo commercials. Drive on to **Zillie Falls** (viewed from above) and **Ellinjaa Falls**.

Detour to Ravenshoe
From Millaa Millaa you could detour southwest 25km (15 miles) on the Old Palmerston Highway to **Raven-shoe ➒**, Queensland's highest town at 920m (3,000ft). The **Ravenshoe Visi-tor Centre** (24 Moore Street; www.trc. qld.gov.au/locations/ravenshoe-visi tor-centre; daily 9am–4pm, until 5pm May–Oct) can help with accommo-dation bookings and information on regional waterfalls and bushwalks. Within the visitor centre is also the **Nganyai Interpretive Centre**, show-casing the culture of the local Jirrbal people, whose language is one of the oldest spoken in the world.

RETURN TO CAIRNS

Homeward bound, take the Palm-erston Highway east towards Innis-fail. After 5km (3 miles) turn left on Brooks Road to **Mungalli Falls**. At the **Mungalli Creek Dairy** (251 Brooks Road, Millaa Millaa; www.mungalli creekdairy.com.au; daily 10am–4pm, closed 1 Feb–14 Mar) you can sam-ple organic milk and cheese, and snack at the café. Brooks Road loops back to the Palmerston High-way, which descends through 14km (8 miles) of lush rainforest. At **Craw-ford's Lookout ➓** there are views through a clearing down to the North Johnstone River, where you may spot white-water rafters. Here too is **Mamu Rainforest Canopy Walkway** (Woo-roonooran National Park; http:// mamutropicalskywalk.com.au; daily 9.30am–5.30pm; charge), where you can perch high amongst the rainforest canopy, looking down at the mighty North Johnstone River. These rainfor-

Mungalli Falls

est-clad mountains have cultural significance to the Mamu people, and informative signs explain the cultural history of the area. The return walk is 2.5km (1.5 miles), but allow at least an hour to enjoy the scenery properly along the 350m (1,150ft) of elevated walkway and from the 37m (120ft)

observation tower with two viewing decks.

From here head 25km (16 miles) east to the Bruce Highway, where it's a straightforward run north for 87km (54 miles) back to Cairns. Alternatively, drive south for Mission Beach (see page 96).

Food and Drink

1 JAQUES COFFEE PLANTATION

137 Leotta Road, Mareeba; tel: 4093 3284; www.jaquescoffee.com.au; daily 10am–4pm; $

Accompany the local brew with a selection of cookies, scones and cake, including tropical fruit cheesecakes. This family-owned coffee plantation also offers tours.

2 TOLGA BAKERY

1/56 Main Street, Tolga; tel: 4095 4720; Mon–Fri 6am–3.30pm, Sat 7am–1pm; $–$$

A wonderful assortment of breads, sandwiches, pies, and sweets, which clearly display the care and attention that goes into making each item on this cosy menu.

3 NICK'S SWISS-ITALIAN RESTAURANT

33 Gillies Highway, Yungaburra; tel: 4095 3330; www.nicksrestaurant.com.au; Sat–Sun 11.30am–2.30pm, Fri–Sat 6.30pm–8.30pm; $$$

Choose from Nick's extensive Swiss-Italian menu, which includes pasta, rosti and Swiss

bratwurst. Or if you prefer modern Australian, try crumbed crocodile fillets or a jackaroo sirloin steak.

4 THE LAKE BARRINE TEAHOUSE RESTAURANT

Lake Barrine, Gillies Highway, Yungaburra; tel: 4095 3847; www.lakebarrine.com.au; daily 9am–4pm; $$

Overlooking the lake, this place serves hearty breakfasts, light lunches, such as soups, salads and sandwiches, and all-day Devonshire teas.

5 SMOKEHOUSE CAFÉ

Australian Platypus Park at Tarzali Lakes, Malanda–Millaa Millaa Road, Malanda; tel: 4097 2713; www.tarzalilakes.com; daily 8am–4pm; $$

Nestled on the shores of a lake stocked with barramundi, golden perch, jade perch and red claw (a delicious crustacean), it comes as no surprise that this café specialises in freshly prepared fish and, of course, a wide range of smoked treats; more surprising, however, is the extensive Thai menu.

Palm trees fringing Mission Beach

MISSION BEACH
AND DUNK ISLAND

The first day of this driving route south of Cairns takes you to picturesque waterfalls on the way to the seaside village of Mission Beach. Day two is spent exploring Dunk Island, a tropical paradise for intrepid travellers.

DISTANCE: 157km (94 miles) from Cairns to Mission Beach
TIME: Two days
START: Cairns
END: Dunk Island
POINTS TO NOTE: On 3 February 2011, Tropical Cyclone Yasi ripped through parts of northern Queensland, leaving a trail of utter devastation in its wake and causing nearly a billion dollars in damage. The eye of the storm passed directly over Mission Beach and Dunk Island. While Mission Beach has largely recovered, and has plenty of accommodation for all budgets, Dunk Island Resort remains in ruins, although there are plans for redevelopment. You can still visit the island as a day-tripper, or stay overnight in a tent – which will appeal to the adventurous, as will the fact that the beautiful island is almost devoid of tourists. You need a car for this route. Pack water and snacks.

As you travel south from Cairns, the route passes through spectacular mountain scenery and fertile fields of bananas and sugarcane to reach Australia's wettest towns. This is part of the 'Great Green Way', and here you will observe ever-increasing tropical greenery and experience the relaxed north Queensland lifestyle, where farming and fishing are dominant ways of life and where a cultural encounter involves having a yarn with locals in an old Queensland pub.

TO MISSION BEACH

Set out early from Cairns, travelling south on the Bruce Highway through Edmonton and Gordonvale. **Babinda**, about 60km (36 miles) south of Cairns, competes annually with Tully and Innisfail for the 'Golden Gumboot Award', which goes to the town recording the highest annual average rainfall, usually around 5m (over 15ft). The locals will tell you it rains for 11 months, and drips off the trees for the rest of the year. In fact, large amounts of rain tend to fall in a very short time, and there is plenty of tropical sunshine to power the unusually lush and diverse vegetation.

Falls in Paronella Park

Babinda Boulders

At Babinda, turn right and follow signs west for 8km (5 miles) to **Babinda Boulders ❶**, a Wet Tropics World Heritage Reserve with visitor facilities, located in the foothills of **Mt Bartle Frere**, Queensland's highest mountain at 1,622m (5,300ft). Take your swimming costume to the Boulders and walk the 850m/yd **Wonga Track Rainforest** path to clear pools amidst giant tree ferns, moss-covered boulders and towering trees. The short **Devils Pool Walk** is a bit more challenging, but also a lovely stroll through the rainforest to viewing platforms and cascading pools. This entire area is a popular swimming spot for locals and tourists, but stick to the marked swimming areas and exercise care, as people have drowned at Devils Pool.

Josephine Falls

Continue south on the Bruce Highway, and after 9km (5.5 miles) take a right turn to **Josephine Falls ❷**. This is an 8km (5-mile) detour from the highway, and 10 minutes' walk through the rainforest will reward you with some of the most beautiful waterfalls in Queensland. The tumbling icy waters have been used in many television commercials, and you can swim here.

Innisfail and Paronella Park

The sugar town of **Innisfail** is another 13km (8 miles) further south. Sitting at the junction of the North Johnstone and South Johnstone rivers, Innisfail is the no-fuss service hub for the region.

From Innisfail, take the Old Bruce Highway (Japoonvale Road) for 18.5km (11.5 miles) to **Paronella Park ❸** (Mena Creek;   www.paronellapark.com.au; daily 9am–8pm; guided walks every 30 minutes 9.30am–4.30pm; night tour 6.15pm; charge). Back in 1913, Jose Paronella dreamt of building a Spanish castle alongside Mena Creek, and by 1935 his dream had been realised. A magnificent castle with grand staircase, lakeside tunnels and bridges, picnic areas and surrounded by gardens was opened to the public. This is a unique spot to enjoy lunch

White-water rafting

Near Tully, in a remote part of the Wet Tropics World Heritage Rainforest, the Tully River snakes through dramatic gorges. Its energy can be experienced on a full-day white-water rafting trip. Along its twisting, scenic descent there are over 45 churning (normally grade 3–4) rapids to conquer on a day packed with action and adventure. No prior experience is necessary, as river guides have intimate knowledge of every bend, curve and drop of the river and rapids. Trips with two main operators, RnR White Water Rafting Adventure (www.raft.com.au) and Raging Thunder   (www.ragingthunder.com.au), are available year-round with transfers from/to your accommodation in Mission Beach, Cairns, Northern Beaches and Port Douglas. You need to be 13 years or older to raft.

On Dunk Island's jetty

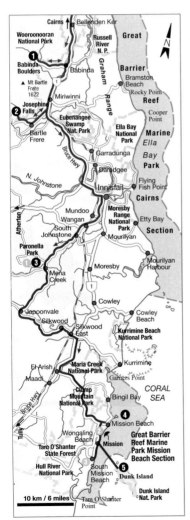

at **Café on the Deck**, see ❶, overlooking Jose's exotic creation.

MISSION BEACH

From Paronella Park, you are about 45 minutes from Mission Beach. Follow the signs south through Japoonvale to Silkwood on the Bruce Highway (23km/14 miles). Turn right onto the highway for **El Arish**, from where you turn left off the highway for the 16km (10-mile) drive to **Mission Beach** ❹. Made up of four communities – **Bingil Bay, Mission Beach** itself, **Wongaling Beach** and **South Mission Beach** – it boasts 14km (8.5 miles) of unspoilt palm-fringed coastline overlooking more than 20 tropical offshore islands dotting the Coral Sea. The area offers a large array of adventure activities, and you will find accommodation for all budgets (see page 111), including camping on Dunk Island (www.dunk-island.com).

Call in at the **Mission Beach Visitor Centre** (Porter Promenade; www.mission beachtourism.com; Mon–Sat 9am–5pm, Sun 10am–2pm), located on the beachfront just outside Mission Beach village on the way to Bingil Bay. Here you'll find information on numerous activities, galleries and accommodation options as well as details on the local mascot, the rare and endangered southern cassowary. Mission Beach is one of the few places where you're likely to see this huge flightless bird.

Being the closest mainland point to the Great Barrier Reef, snorkelling and scuba-diving trips are popular and offer

White water rafting on the Tully River

a much quieter and less crowded option than those in Cairns. If you like your diving to be faster and less wet, try skydiving. Mission Beach is one of the most spectacular drop zones in the country. Check out Jump the Beach (www.jumpthebeach.com.au) for some serious thrills.

For a sleepy seaside town, Mission Beach has a surprising selection of sophisticated restaurants and eateries. **Nana Thai Cafe**, see ②, offers a fantastic dining experience. There are no eating options open on Dunk Island at the time of writing, but **Dunk Island View Caravan Park Café**, see ③, offers views of the island and wonderful fish and chips.

DUNK ISLAND

Offshore, the Family Group of Islands beckon. The most northerly, **Dunk Island** ⑤, just 4km (2.5 miles) out to sea, was once a main attraction here, but Cyclone Yasi knocked the island around badly, and now it's only hardy types who visit. The **water taxi** (Banfield Parade, Wongaling; www.missionbeachwatertaxi.com) still takes people to the island – a 10-minute crossing – three times a day (9am, 10am and 11am, returning 12pm and 3.30pm). Note that in order to board, you need to wade through shallow water. **Coral Sea Kayaking** (2 Wall Street, South Mission Beach; www.coralseakayaking.com) offer guided kayak trips to the island, including lunch and leisure time.

Dunk is a beautiful rainforested island offering 13km (8 miles) of walking track taking in most of the island's lovely and secluded beaches.

Food and Drink

① CAFÉ ON THE DECK

Paronella Park, Japoonvale Road (Old Bruce Highway), Mena Creek; tel: 4065 0000; www.paronellapark.com.au; daily breakfast and lunch; $
Enjoy a light lunch on the outdoor deck consisting of sandwiches, focaccias, pies or their celebrated homemade jam and scones.

② NANA THAI CAFE

165 Reid Rd, Wongaling Beach; tel: 4068 9101; www.millersbeachbar.com.au; Tue–Sat 5pm–8.30pm; $
Reasonably-priced Thai dishes and quick service. Family owned and a sporting a wonderful beach front location.

③ DUNK ISLAND VIEW CARAVAN PARK AND CAFÉ

21-35 Webb Road, Mission Beach; tel: 4068 8248; Tue–Wed 7.30am–4pm, Thu–Mon 7.30am–8pm; $
You might not be able to go and order a meal on Dunk Island at the moment, but you can enjoy some of the region's best fish and chips at this fantastic café with a view of the island. Also serves highly rated coffee.

DIRECTORY

Hand-picked hotels and restaurants to suit all budgets and tastes, organised by area, plus select nightlife listings, an alphabetical listing of practical information, a language guide and an overview of the best books and films to give you a flavour of the city.

Stamford Plaza Hotel is located by the Brisbane River

ACCOMMODATION

Coastal Queensland has a huge range of accommodation options, and you are unlikely to have any difficulty finding a place to stay unless there is a major event in progress when you plan to visit. Boutique rural retreats, hotels and hostels across inland areas, such as the Atherton Tablelands, are also becoming more popular, and self-catering cabins are always an interesting option to explore. When booking hotel accommodation, there is some latitude for striking a deal for longer stays, weekend rates, standby rates and so on. Check for internet-only rates, and it is always worth asking about 'specials' when speaking directly to the hotel. The vast majority of hotels have rooms for non-smokers, so request these when booking.

Brisbane

Banana Bender Backpackers

118 Petrie Terrace; tel: 3367 1157; www.bananabenders.com; $

Only a short bus ride from the city centre, this popular hostel has a range of room options, including female-only dorms and double and twin rooms. The fan-cooled rooms are kept clean, and Bananas also offer airport shuttle service, internet access and backpacker party nights.

Brisbane City YHA

392 Upper Roma Street; tel: 3236 1004; www.yha.com.au; $

This convenient hostel – a winner of the Best Backpacker Accommodation, Queensland Tourism Awards – is close to the Brisbane Transit Centre and to Caxton Street's fabulous nightlife. Rooms are either three-share or doubles, and all are air-conditioned. There's a good café, rooftop pool, games room full of electronic games, and a very helpful travel and tour desk.

Emporium Hotel South Bank

267 Grey St.; tel: 3556 3333; www.emporiumhotels.com.au; $$$$

A Bohemian-style luxury boutique hotel, has 143 rooms with several design flourishes that leave an impression, and the Piano Bar, which sports a decadent menu and an extensive selection of drinks. Rooms are equally as deluxe.

Lucerne on Fernberg

23 Fernberg Road, Paddington; tel: 3369 6686; www.lucerne.net.au; $$

A heritage-listed B&B in what is believed to be the oldest privately owned building in Queensland. The beautifully

> Price for a double room for one night without breakfast:
> $$$$ = over A$220
> $$$ = A$150–220
> $$ = A$80–150
> $ = below A$80

A room with a view at the Stamford Plaza

presented accommodation is in the separate Coach House or Rose Cottage (the latter accessible for people in wheelchairs); both with mini home-theatre systems and cooking facilities. BBQ, parking and laundry facilities are available, and guests are welcome to enjoy the lovely wraparound veranda and gardens.

Pullman Brisbane King George Square

Corner of Ann and Roma streets; tel: 3229 9111; www.accorhotels.com; $$$$

Formerly the Sebel King George Square Hotel, the rooms here strike a tidy balance between the needs of the holiday maker and the business guest - both of whom will appreciate the central location, views over King George Square and various luxury touches. Excellent facilities include parking, pool, restaurants and bar.

The Great Southern Hotel Brisbane

103 George Street; tel: 3221 6044; https://greatsouthernhotel.com.au; $$

Formerly the Rendezvous Studio Hotel on George, this modern boutique hotel is less than five minutes' walk from the city, casino or the river. It boasts excellent service and three grades of rooms, with the top-of-the-range spa suites overlooking the river and South Bank. Facilities include a heated outdoor pool, gymnasium, restaurant and bar, and undercover parking.

Rydges Southbank Hotel

9 Glenelg Streets, Southbank; tel: 3364 0800; www.rydges.com; $$$$

Location, location, location. Right near the South Bank Parklands and cultural precinct, with hundreds of rooms ranging over several categories, this five-star hotel can have great-value room deals on the internet. There are bars and restaurants, but you also have the great restaurants on Grey and Little Stanley streets nearby.

Spicers Balfour Hotel

37 Balfour Street, Brisbane; tel: 1300 597 540; www.spicersgroup.com.au; $$$$

With its uniquely designed rooms, complemented by a communal library and a rooftop bar (serving sublime food) this European style boutique hotel is in New Farm, close to a wide variety of restaurants and overlooking the Brisbane River. This is the perfect place to escape the city.

Stamford Plaza Hotel

Corner Margaret & Edward streets; tel: 3221 1999; www.stamford.com.au; $$$$

An elegant and contemporary hotel with a lovely heritage facade, located on the bank of the Brisbane River. All 252 rooms in this modern high-rise building boast panoramic river views and are comfortable and spacious.

Treasury Casino and Hotel

130 William Street; tel: 3306 8888; www.treasurybrisbane.com.au; $$$$

An award-winning hotel located in the grand former Land Administration build-

A bright apartment at the Tangalooma Island Resort

ing, ideally situated in the heart of Brisbane with views of the river and South Bank across the street. Ornate and sumptuous heritage furnishings accentuate the hotel's opulent character, and the casino provides several dining and entertainment options.

Pacific Hotel Brisbane

345 Wickham Terrace; tel: 3831 6177; https://pacifichotelbrisbane.com.au; $$
Centrally located and surrounded by parklands, the boutique Pacific has comfortable if simple rooms with small private balconies. The in-house Gazebo restaurant and bar offers relaxed dining with a 'fusion' menu – al fresco on the balcony, or inside – and the place has a touch of class. Pool and gym access is available to guests.

Moreton Island

Blue Ocean View Beach House

Tangalooma, Moreton Island; tel: 408 870 694; http://blueoceanviewbeachhouse.com; $$$
For fans of self-catering, this luxury beach house overlooking Moreton Bay and Tangalooma - the former whaling station where dolphins are now common visitors - is a slice of private luxury. With three bedrooms, two bathrooms and a deck, the house is spacious and fully kitted out, plus it's only a 60-minute ride on the Micat or Tangalooma Flyer from Brisbane. You even get to use the 6-seat electric golf buggy, for free.

Tangalooma Island Resort

tel: 1300 652 250; www.tangalooma.com; $$$$
This efficient all-in-one, eco-friendly, family-focused resort offers numerous packages that include activities and tours such as the famous dolphin feeding at dusk. Choose between hotel rooms, serviced apartments, villa units and fully self-contained houses with various levels of comforts and luxury. There are several beachside restaurants for casual dining.

Sunshine Coast

10 Hastings Street Boutique Motel & Café

10 Hastings Street; tel: 1300 130 698; www.10hastingsstreet.com.au; $$
Formerly the Noosa Village Motel, this intimate venue has undergone a A$1.5 million refurbishment, and has good, bright apartment suites and studios. The position, at the quieter end of Noosa's happening Hastings Street, close to Main Beach is perfect for both landscape leering and people watching. Great café too.

Mantra French Quarter Resort

62 Hastings Street, Noosa Heads; tel: 13 15 17; www.mantra.com.au; $$$
Right on Noosa's main drag and only 50m/yds from the beach, rooms here are either one- or two-bedroom apartments with kitchenette and balcony overlooking Hastings Street with all its fine eateries, or the landscaped gardens with a lagoon-style pool.

Looking over Noosa's prime location

Halse Lodge

2 Halse Lane, Noosa Heads; tel: 5447 3377; www.yha.com.au/hostels/qld/sunshine-coast/noosa-heads; $

This backpackers' retreat and YHA hostel is in a rambling old Queenslander surrounded by rainforest gardens with the surf beach only 100m/yds away. As well as dorms there are twin and double rooms and a restaurant and bar. Very popular, so book ahead.

North Stradbroke Island

Manta Lodge YHA

132 Dickson Way, Point Lookout, North Stradbroke Island; 3409 8888; www.mantalodge.com.au; $

Perched right on the beachfront on gorgeous North Stradbroke Island, not only is this a super-friendly hostel offering superb value budget accommodation, it's also a 5-Star PADI dive resort offering daily scuba dive and snorkel trips. Marine highlights here include manta rays encounters and shark dives with grey nurse sharks.

Stradbroke Island Beach Hotel and Spa Resort

158 East Coast Road, Point Lookout; tel: 3409 8188; www.stradbrokehotel.com.au; $$$

Situated atop a headland and overlooking pristine beaches where you may glimpse a whale, the 'Straddie Pub' offers ocean-facing apartments plus hotel rooms and suites. Minimum-stay rules typically apply, and a potential drawback – or plus – is that the popular

bar and restaurant keep the action busy and the noise levels high until midnight.

Gold Coast

Coolangatta YHA

230 Coolangatta Road, Bilinga; tel: 5536 7644; www.coolangattayha.com; $

Only 500m/yds from Coolangatta Airport and 150m/yds from the amazing surf of North Kirra Beach. Rooms range from dorms to singles, doubles and family rooms. Tour bookings, surfboard hire, surfing lessons and shuttles to the best breaks are all available. To say that this friendly hostel is surf-obsessed would be an understatement.

Novotel Surfers Paradise

Corner of Surfers Paradise Boulevard and Hanlan Street, Surfers Paradise; tel: 5579 3499; www.accorhotels.com/gb/hotel-A7P0-novotel-surfers-paradise/index.shtml; $$$

It's just 150 metres from the door of your hotel to the sand of Surfers here. Rooms have private balconies, so all you need to do is choose between an ocean or a city skyline view. Facilities include a pool and spa, and great seafood is served at Hanlan's restaurant and bar.

Hill Haven Holiday Apartments

2 Goodwin Terrace, Burleigh Heads; tel: 5535 1055; www.hillhaven.com.au; $$$

Nestled into the headland and adjoining Burleigh Heads National Park, this block of spacious apartments is superbly positioned with restaurants and a renowned surf beach just a short

stroll away. Beautifully furnished two- and three-bedroom apartments offer panoramic views over Surfers Paradise, the ocean and the hinterland from balconies. The three-night booking minimum in the low season rises to five nights in the holiday season. The views will take your breath away.

Oaks Calypso Plaza Resort
99 Griffith Street, Coolangatta; tel: 1300 662 293; www.oakshotelsresorts.com/oaks-calypso-plaza; $$
An attractive, family-friendly, low-rise well away from the high-rise strip, very near the surf beach and airport. This well thought-out resort is equipped with a gym, games room and a lagoon-style swimming pool. Rooms range from studios to one- and two-bedroom apartments. They regularly offer specials, so be sure to ask when you book.

Palazzo Versace
94 Sea World Drive, Main Beach; tel: 5509 8000; www.palazzoversace.com; $$$$
The ultimate in 'Renaissance' splendour, luxury and immaculate service is expressed in this 205-room hotel, the first venture into hotels by Donatella Versace. Supposedly a six-star establishment, it has all the style and extravagance associated with the brand liberally embossed throughout.

Pelican Cove
6 Back St., at Back and Burrows streets, Surfers Paradise; tel: 5537 7001; www.pelicancove.com.au; $$
This family-friendly resort has self-contained two- and three-bedroom units right on the Broadwater waterfront, a tennis court, saltwater swimming pools, and spacious grounds. Just 10 minutes from Wet 'n' Wild, Dreamworld, Sea World and Movie World theme parks, and the tour desk sells discounted tickets.

Gold Coast hinterland
Binna Burra Mountain Lodge
Lamington National Park; tel: 5533 3622; www.binnaburralodge.com.au; $$$
Perched on a hinterland ridge with sweeping views, this award-winning eco-lodge is a romantic retreat, offering log cabins with dinner, bed and breakfast, or just bed-and-breakfast packages. There are also campsites available, plus a restaurant, spa and nature trails. Certified by the EcoTourism Australia board.

O'Reilly's Rainforest Retreat
3582 Lamington National Park Road, via Canungra; tel: 1 800 688 722; www.oreillys.com.au; $$$$
The choice is simple here at this beautiful spot on the edge of the Lamington National Park: a mountain villas with all mod cons, including designer decor, high-def LCD TV, rooms opening onto expansive private decks with outdoor spa bath and BBQ, or a complete digital detox in one of the Rainforest Retreats, which deliberately do

High-rises frame Main Beach on the Gold Coast

not feature telephones or televisions, but which do boast king-size four-poster beds, en suite bathrooms and a couples' spa. The Canopy Suites also have open fireplaces. Minimum stay of two nights. Check their website for directions on how to get there because many smartphone maps will take you in the wrong direction.

Fraser Island

Kingfisher Bay Resort
PMB 1 Urangan Hervey Bay; tel: 4120 3333; www.kingfisherbay.com; $$$
A well-appointed eco-resort that has island-based hotel rooms, self-contained villas surrounded by rainforest, and multi-bedroom houses. The better rooms have sea views and spa baths. There are four swimming pools, four bars and four restaurants, and the resort has a helpful tour and activity desk.

Whitsunday Islands and Airlie Beach

Airlie Beach Hotel
At The Esplanade and Coconut Grove, Airlie Beach; tel: 4964 1999; www.airliebeachhotel.com.au; $$–$$$$
A prime seafront location with four-star facilities makes this one of the busier hotels in town, but justifiably so. Hotel rooms have either beach-view or town-view balconies and sleep either two or three people. Less expensive, three-star motel rooms do not have the balcony views. Mangrove Jack's Café/Bar

is on site, offering quality casual dining options and pub favourites, and the main drag is only a stroll away.

Coral Sea Resort
25 Oceanview Avenue, Airlie Beach; tel: 4964 1300; www.coralsearesort.com; $$$
The only absolute waterfront resort in Airlie Beach offers a range of apartment-style rooms, many with spa baths, near the Abel Point marina. The resort is just three minutes' stroll along a boardwalk from Airlie Beach's main drag. The setting is stunning, with a large pool, great patio café and bar, and the resort's own jetty doubles as a dining venue. The rooms range from one-bedroom hotel rooms to suites, apartments and penthouses.

Hamilton Island
Tel: 9007 0009; www.hamiltonisland.com.au; $$$$
A range of room types are available on this highly developed, self-contained island – and all of them are expensive. Choose from the exclusive Qualia, Beach Club, Reef View Hotel, the Palm Bungalows, Holidays Homes, or the Yacht Club Villas. There's a staggering range of recreation and dining options, too.

Magnums Backpackers
366 Shute Harbour Road, Airlie Beach; tel: 4964 6188; www.magnums.com.au; $
The most central hostel at Airlie is also one of the friendliest. It offers dormi-

Brisbane's river skyline

tory, twin share and double accommodation, and the cheapest beer in town. There's a helpful tour desk, and it is right across the road from the swimming lagoon.

Reef Sleep

ReefWorld, Great Barrier Reef, off Hamilton Island; tel: 4846 7000; www.cruisewhitsundays.com/gbra-Reefsleep.aspx; $$$$

Slumber under the stars on the roof of a pontoon in the midst of the Great Barrier Reef, being rocked to sleep by the gentle movement of the Coral Sea while you snuggle into the most Australian of all inventions: the swag (a cross between a sleeping bag and a tent). This is a new offering from Cruise Whitsundays, and besides an al fresco sleeping experience you'll also enjoy 5-star hospitality (meals served in an underwater chamber looking out on the reef) and a chance to go night diving before you turn in for the night.

Cairns

Acacia Court Hotel

223–227 The Esplanade; tel: 4051 5011; www.acaciacourt.com: $$

The Acacia Court Hotel is just 2km (1.25 miles) from the city centre, a pleasant walk along The Esplanade. Rooms have queen-size beds, en suite bath or shower rooms, and balconies with either ocean or mountain views. There are also cheaper motel-style rooms. The on-site restaurant

Charlie's has an all-you-can-eat buffet every night.

Cairns Central YHA

20-26 McLeod Street; tel: 4051 0772; www.yha.com.au/hostels/qld/cairns-and-far-north-queensland/cairns-backpackers-hostel; $

A large and buzzing youth hostel, complete with a welcoming swimming pool to dive into when the tropical heat gets a little too much to bear. The YHA is centrally located and has plenty of communal facilities, including internet facilitates and a laundry. Get up early and you can blag yourself a share of the free pancakes that are cooked and handed out each morning. Family rooms are also available.

Galvins Edge Hill B&B

61 Walsh Street; tel: 4032 1308; www.galvinsonedge.com.au; $$$

This welcoming B&B is in a genuine old Queenslander in a peaceful location. With a lounge and breakfast room that opens onto the natural-rock swimming pool, and just two bedrooms and a bathroom, only one family or group is booked at a time, so you have the whole place to yourselves.

Gilligan's Backpackers Hotel and Resort

57–89 Grafton Street; tel: 4041 6566; www.gilligansbackpackers.com.au; $

This huge and often raucous backpackers' resort offers economical

Treasury Casino and Hotel   *An elegant Treasury hotel room*

dorm beds plus twin and double rooms, rowdy entertainment and a social soup of a swimming pool. All rooms are air-conditioned and have en suite bathrooms, and each floor has its own kitchen. Guests get free airport transfers.

Shangri-La Hotel
The Marina, Pier Point Road; tel: 4031 1411; www.shangri-la.com/cairns; $$$$
Fronting the turquoise waters of Trinity Inlet and the Marlin Marina with its bobbing luxury flotilla, this luxury hotel has excellent views and a convenient location. Rooms and suites boast private balconies or patios and a range of leisure facilities, including a large swimming pool, in more than an acre of lush tropical gardens.

Palm Cove

Hotel Grand Chancellor Palm Cove
Coral Coast Drive, Palm Cove; tel: 4059 1234; www.grandchancellorhotels.com/au/palmcove; $$
Perfect for travelling families, this resort has a games room and not one but two swimming pools, one boasting watersides and other small-person crowd pleasing features. For bigger guests there's a bar, alfresco dining area and various pampering facilities. It's only 5 minutes' walk to the beach.

The Reef Retreat
10–14 Harpa Street Palm Cove; tel: 4059 1744; www.reefretreat.com.au; $$
Just across from the beach at Palm Cove, Reef Retreat offers a lovely low-rise alternative to those who don't want the big hotel experience. Accommodation is in a collection of self-contained boutique apartments set in a verdant rainforest setting, complete with refreshing pool, a spa and communal BBQs. Owners couldn't be more friendly and welcoming.

Sebel Reef House & Spa
99 Williams Esplanade; tel: 4080 2600; www.reefhouse.com.au; $$$$
Much-heralded boutique property just opposite the beach at Palm Cove. Its bygone-era Queensland architecture is truly charming, with 67 oversized rooms and suites accented by wooden shutters, terracotta floors, wicker furniture and mosquito nets draped over beds. Lush gardens, a courtyard pool and a delightful restaurant complete the picture.

Port Douglas

Hibiscus Gardens Spa Resort
22 Owens Street; tel: 4099 5315; http://www.hibiscusresortandspa.com.au; $$$
Set among exotic gardens with two pools, this neat hotel has a Balinese theme. Accommodation spans motel-style to three-bedroom apartments, some with private spas. And it is less than five minutes' walk to the beach and shops.

Palazzo Versace's opulent style

Rendezvous Reef Resort

121 Port Douglas Road; tel 4087 2790; https://reefresortportdouglas.com.au; $$

Sprawling cross 15 acres of lush tropical gardens, this resort is one for water babies, boasting two lagoon-style pools, one leisure pool, one 25-metre lap pool (with eight lanes) and one children's pool - and of course the beach is only across the road. A short stroll out of town, the Port Douglas Shuttle runs every 15 minutes will give you a ride if it's too hot to walk. Rooms are modern and clean, many are split level with balconies overlooking the pools.

Sheraton Mirage Port Douglas Resort

Port Douglas Road; tel: 4099 5888; www.sheratonportdouglas.com; $$$$

Almost 300 rooms and over 100 villas circle an epic swimming lagoon in this sprawling 130-hectare resort, a stretch of luxurious greenery that spoons Four Mile Beach for several hundred metres. You can access the beach from the resort, perfect for sunrise and sunset wanders along the sand into town. The bar and restaurant are under cover, but with views out across the property.

Daintree and Cape Tribulation

Cape Tribulation Beach House Resort

152 Rykers Road, Cape Tribulation; tel: 4098 0030; www.capetribbeach.com.au; $–$$$

Situated 48km (30 miles) from the ferry terminal, this place provides dormitory and family cabins across eight price categories to cater for all budgets. Common areas include the saltwater swimming pool, the Sand Bar and Bistro, and communal kitchen and laundry facilities for self-caterers. It is located as close to the beach as the National Parks Authority will allow.

Daintree Eco Lodge & Spa

20 Daintree Road, Daintree; tel: 4777 7377; www.daintree-ecolodge.com.au; $$$$

Just 15 private cabins are offered at this eco-luxury nature retreat nestled into the rainforest a short drive from Daintree village. It's not one for families, but a great romantic splurge with a wellbeing spa and a restaurant that takes cues from the local environment and indigenous knowledge to create its Australian tropical cuisine.

Ferntree Rainforest Lodge

36 Camelot Close, Cape Tribulation; tel: 4098 0000; www.ferntreerainforestlodge.com.au; $$

There's a large selection of accommodation options here, ranging from budget dorm rooms right through to split-level cabins set in the rainforest garden, pool-side suites with balconies looking over a lagoon, and secluded private cabins. The Cassowary Café serves a good selection of food daily and the owners can also help arrange tours.

Cairns' Shangri-La Hotel

Atherton Tablelands

Barking Owl Retreat

409 Hough Road, Kairi, Atherton Tablelands; tel: 4095 8455; www.barkingowlretreat.com.au; $$$

Stay a night or two in the so-much-friendlier-than-it-sounds 'Dingo's Lair', and experience the Atherton Tablelands as they should be seen, from a verandah with only the sounds of the bush to interrupt your reverie. The property boasts a dam where you can fish (and release), or sit chatting around the fire pit, and your hosts are friendly and knowledgeable.

Cedar Park Rainforest Resort

250 Cedarpark Road, Kuranda; tel: 4093 7892; www.cedarparkresort.com.au; $$

Somewhere between Kuranda and Mareeba, up on the Atherton Tablelands, you'll find this spellbinding place. With just five rooms, set in an idyllic rainforest environment full of wildlife, it's run by super-friendly Swiss ex-pats, who will spoil you rotten. The layout of the place is eccentric, which adds to the charm, and among its many great features is an al fresco restaurant overlooking the Wet Tropics World Heritage Rainforest. Dinner is served every night, whenever you want it.

Eden House Retreat and Mountain Spa

20 Gillies Highway, Yungaburra; tel: 4089 7000; www.edenhouse.com.au; $$$

This exquisite heritage retreat offers secluded cottages and villas with private spas set in luxuriant gardens. Although aimed at couples looking for a relaxing escape (four-poster safari-style beds included), there is adequate accommodation for families as well. There's a restaurant and bar and the excellent Mountain Spa that offers a wide range of indulgent packages to pamper your body and soul.

Mission Beach

The Elandra at Mission Beach

41 Explorer Drive, South Mission Beach; tel: 4068 8154; www.elandraresorts.com; $$$–$$$$

The views from this resort-style hotel, on the southern headland above Mission Beach, are magnificent. The luxury accommodation with its chic African tribal theme is set amidst rainforest rich in wildlife, and the building is architecturally designed so that everybody enjoys privacy and an elevated ocean and beach view.

Sejala on the Beach

26 Pacific Parade, Mission Beach; 455 898 699; www.sejala.com.au; $$$$

Choose between three beautiful boutique beachfront huts (en suite and complete with air-con and beachfront verandahs), tucked away in a tropical garden and just metres away from one of the world's best beaches, or the big, spacious beach house. Facilities to tempt you out of your hammock include a private in-house glass tiled terrace pool set amid pink ginger, mandevillea and lime trees.

RESTAURANTS

In Brisbane and Cairns and along the coast where tourism is significant, you will have no trouble finding quality fresh food prepared with flair – and usually with multicultural influences. In Brisbane, there are several restaurant neighbourhoods just a few minutes' cab drive or bus/ferry ride from the CBD (see page 17), while in Cairns, Shields Street is known as 'Eats Street', with more dining options along the boardwalk facing the Marlin Marina and along the Esplanade. On the islands around the reef, the fact that resort-based restaurants basically have you at their mercy can sometimes mean that prices are high, but the quality should also be top notch – their reputation as a destination depends on it.

The foundation of Australian cuisine is the quality and variety of its ingredients. Locally sourced produce, meats and fish are highly sought after. Aussies were slow to recognise the wealth of seafood in their waters, but now a range of fresh fish is on every menu. Small farms devote themselves to gourmet beef and poultry, while the quality of everyday vegetables rivals that grown on organic farms in Europe or the United States. Far from pining for imports of French cheese, Greek olives or Italian wine, Australians produce their own, which are often rated superior to the imports.

Australia can be divided into regions that are known for particular produce and each state has its acknowledged specialities. In the case of tropical Queensland, they are the wealth of exotic fruits, like Bowen mangoes and papaya, as well as succulent reef fish, mudcrabs and Moreton Bay bugs (see page 16).

Brisbane

Alchemy Restaurant and Bar

175 Eagle Street; tel: 3229 3175; www.alchemyrestaurant.com.au; Mon–Fri 12–3pm, 6–10pm; Sat 6pm–10pm; $$$

A Brisbane favourite for many years, the Alchemy's beef cheeks are legendary, but the European-flavoured menu is eclectic and sophisticated, and includes a wonderful cheese list. The location, right by the Brisbane River overlooking the Story Bridge, just adds spice to the experience.

Aria Restaurant

Eagle Street Pier, 1 Eagle Street; tel: 3233 2555; www.ariarestaurant.com.au; Tue–Thu 5.30pm–10pm, Fri 12pm–2.30pm and 5.30pm–10pm, Sat 5pm–10pm; $$$

Also with spectacular views over Story Bridge and the Brisbane River, Aria has an elegant contemporary menu devised by

Price range for a two-course meal for one including a glass of house wine:
$$$=over A$60
$$=A$40–60
$=below $40

The dining room at Aria

celebrity chef Matt Moran. Seafood and top-quality steaks dominate, but there are vegetarian options and delicate Asian interpretations. The innovative cuisine is matched to an extensive wine list, showcasing many of Australia's iconic wineries.

One Fifty Ascot Bar & Eatery

150 Racecourse Road; tel: 3123 7123; www.onefiftyascot.com.au; Tue–Sat 11.30am–11.45pm; $$$

This location has seen quite a bit of turnover in recent years but the latest incarnation has brought about a new and modern interior to this historic venue. The menu is very good with treats such as pumpkin tortellini with almond and feta and Szechuan calamari.

Breakfast Creek Hotel

2 Kingsford Smith Drive, Albion; tel: 3262 5988; www.breakfastcreekhotel.com; daily noon–2.30pm, 6–10.30pm; $$

The 'Brekkie's' steaks are virtually the size of a dinner plate, and consistently thick, juicy and flavoursome. Choose your own from 12 premium cuts at the barbecue in the Beer Garden or visit the Spanish Garden Steakhouse for full table service and other menu items. But it's the steaks that make this place famous.

Cha Cha Char Wine Bar and Grill

Shop 5 Plaza Level, Eagle Street Pier; tel: 3211 9944; www.chachachar.com.au; Mon–Fri noon–11pm, Sat–Sun 6–11pm; $$$

If you still have not succumbed to Queensland's obsession with succulent steaks, here is the place to give in to temptation. The menu will make you an instant expert in all things steak. Digest the facts about breeding, feed, location and age before devouring the subject. Booking is recommended.

E'cco

63 Skyring Terrace; tel: 3831 8344; www.eccobistro.com; Tue–Sat noon–3pm and 5.30pm until late; $$$

A multi-award winning bistro, thanks to Philip Johnson's simple philosophy: 'Real food, honest food, using the best local produce'. Settle in for field mushrooms, olive toast, rocket and parmesan, or try rare-seared Wagyu beef salad with Asian herbs, chilli caramel and candied sesame seeds. And that's just for starters. Mains on an ever-evolving menu currently include offerings such as roast duck breast, pear, sour cherry and pine nut tarte tatin.

Gambaro's Seafood Restaurant

33 Caxton Street, Petrie Terrace, Paddington; tel: 3369 9500; www.gambaros.com.au; Mon–Thu 11.30am-10pm, Fri until 11pm, Sat 5.30–11pm; $$$

The Gambaro family have been in the seafood business since 1953, and Gambaro's has been a Brisbane institution since it opened in 1972. The seafood platters are a gastronomic delight, and from the tanks you can select Moreton Bay bugs, lobster and mud crabs. While seafood is what the restaurant specialises in, there are other options, including steak, chicken and pasta dishes.

Aria's fine seafood

Gerard's Bistro

Shop 14, 15 James Street Fortitude Valley; tel: 3852 3822; www.gerardsbistro.com.au; daily 6pm–late, Tue–Sun 12pm–3pm; $$

Since opening in July 2012, this James Street venue has been getting tongues flapping and stomachs rumbling. Head Chef, Ben Williamson, has a solid reputation based on past glories (at *Cha Cha Char* and *Urbane*) and in his creations you can taste influences from all around the Mediterranean, Northern Africa, and the Middle East. Try the pigeon breast with beetroot and raspberries or the Boer goat tagine.

Hatch and Co

Gasworks Plaza; tel: 3257 2969; www.hatchandco.com.au; daily 11.30am–10pm; $$$

Braden White, the man in charge of the knives at this chilled out venue in Newstead's stylish Gasworks Plaza, is a highly rated young chef. He is a disciple of traditional slow cooking techniques, and utilises local and sustainable produce to turn out hearty fare including pizzas and share plates – try the pork cheek or the barramundi with crispy artichoke.

Il Centro Restaurant

Eagle Street Pier, Eagle Street; tel: 3221 6090; www.il-centro.com.au; Mon–Fri 12pm–3pm and 5.30pm–10pm, Sat 5.30pm–10pm, Sun 12pm–3pm and 5.30pm–9pm; $$$

Il Centro is one of a trio of quality restaurants overlooking the Brisbane River at the Eagle Street Pier complex. Executive chef Catherine Anders marries Italian recipes with Queensland produce with flair. Expect wonderful seafood and pasta – try the celebrated lasagne *alla granseola* (sand crab lasagne) – plus prime cuts of steak.

Jade Buddha

Eagle Street Pier, 14/1 Eagle Street; tel: 3221 2888; www.jadebuddha.com.au; daily 11.30am–late; $$$

With its Asian-fusion cuisine using plenty of fresh seafood, plus colourful cocktails in the trendy Shadow Lounge, the 'Buddha' attracts Brisbane's glitterati. There are plenty of moreish bar snacks and light meals to kick the night off while feasting on excellent river and bridge views. Try the seafood laksa, chicken katsu curry or the Balinese-style lamb.

Moda Restaurant

61 Petrie Terrace; tel: 3221 7655; www.modarestaurant.com.au; Wed–Sun 11.30am–midnight, Tue 3.30pm–midnight; $$

Chef Javier Codina blends local ingredients with inspiration from his Catalonian homeland and *Moda* is famous for its Pica Pica lunches (an eclectic mix of five Spanish inspired dishes plus café con dulces) and paella Fridays. At other times get stuck into quality French Italian and Catalan cuisine, with tasty plates such as lamb adobo and ocean trout *ballotine* with goat's curd and salmon caviar.

Riverbar and Kitchen

Riparian Plaza, Promenade Level, 71

E'cco restaurant in Brisbane

Eagle Street; tel: 3211 9020; www.
riverbarandkitchen.com.au; daily 7am–
midnight; $

Drop in (you can't book), order at the bar, sit back and drink in the views of the Story Bridge while sipping a quality coffee, and wait for the goodness to arrive in this bright and relaxed riverside joint. Breakfasts to see you right through the day include baked eggs, black pudding, spicy tomato, spinach and flatbread, while later on crack open a bottle of King Valley Pinot Grigio and tuck into a plate of chili salt squid with coriander and lime.

Navala Churrascaria

123 Eagle Street; tel: 3221 3888, http://
navala.com.au; Mon–Fri 12pm–3.30pm and
5.30pm to late, Sat–Sun 12pm–3.30pm and
5pm to late; $$–$$$

Opened in 2014, this is Brazilian BBQ at its finest. Choose from a wide variety of grilled meat cooked using traditional Brazilian methods and enjoy with exceptional river views.

Urbane

181 Mary Street; tel: 3229 2271; www.
urbanerestaurant.com; Thu–Sat 6pm–
midnight; $$$

This is a regular winner of some of the most prestigious Australian food and restaurant awards. The chefs consider evolution to be an important part of any restaurant menu and it is not possible to say that Urbane incorporates one style over another. A meal here consists of something that you have never experienced before.

Julius Pizzeria

77 Grey Street, South Brisbane; tel: 3844
2655; http://juliuspizzeria.com.au; Tue–Wed
noon–9.30pm, Thu until 10pm, Fri–Sat until
10.30pm, Sun until 9.30pm; $$

Simply put they serve some of the most delicious wood-fired pizzas and traditional Italian meals in Brisbane. As such it can be difficult to decide between pasta and pizza. For many couples sometimes the solution is to have each person order one and share. Their specialty cocktails are a good way to complement your meal.

Sunshine Coast

Bistro C

49 Hastings Street, Noosa Heads; tel: 5447
2855; www.bistroc.com.au; daily 7.30am–
11.30pm; $$$

This chic beachside restaurant epitomises the modern Australian dining scene, with an imaginative menu fusing the tastes of the Mediterranean and Asia with Australia's bounty of fresh ingredients. There are five separate, regularly changing menus throughout the day, which offer a wide-ranging selection from coconut chicken salad to caramelised pork belly.

Gold Coast

BSKT Café

4 Lavarack Road, Mermaid Beach; tel; 5526
6565; www.bskt.com.au; Sun 7am–5pm,

Much 'Mod Oz' fare focusses on seafood

Mon–Thu 7am–4pm, Sat–Sun until 10pm; $
This breakfast spot offers a range of options including gluten-free and vegetarian. In their loft they also offer semi-regular yoga classes.

The Broadbeach Tavern
Oasis Shopping Centre, Old Burleigh Road, Broadbeach; tel: 5538 4111; www.broadbeachtavern.com.au; daily 11.30am–8.30pm; $
Choose simple, good-quality meals from a small and inexpensive menu including items such as burgers, fish and chips, and juicy steaks. The tavern is an unpretentious place where guest bands enliven the atmosphere most nights.

Omeros Brothers Seafood Restaurant
Marina Mirage, Seaworld Drive, Main Beach; tel: 5591 7222; www.omerosbros.com; Sun–Thu 12pm-9.30pm, Sat–Sun until 10pm; $$$
Omeros Brothers have been operating award winning restaurants for more than 40 years. They combine a simple but extensive menu with a casual setting right on the boardwalk. Highlights include the Moreton Bay bug's tails.

Ristorante Fellini
Marina Mirage, Seaworld Drive, Main Beach; tel: 5531 0300; www.fellini.com.au; daily noon–10pm; $$–$$$
Brothers Carlo and Tony Percuoco dish up superb Italian cuisine at their elegant, award-winning restaurant. Try the pasta *linguette allo zafferano* – saffron-infused long flat pasta cooked with Moreton Bay bug. The restaurant looks across the Southport Broadwater.

Edgewater Dining & Lounge
Shop 3 G7, Capri on Via Roma, Via Roma, Surfers Paradise; tel: 5570 1624; https://edgewaterdining.com.au; daily 7.30am–midnight; $$$
Killer views out over the ocean waves through their ceiling-high windows. For breakfast you can't go wrong with their fresh juices or any of the farm-fresh egg dishes. For dinner, choose from their specialty burgers, pastas or oysters.

Shuck
20 Tedder Avenue, Main Beach; tel: 5528 4286; http://shuck.com.au; daily noon–late; $$$
As the name implies, Shuck is noted for oysters, along with excellent seafood chowder, bouillabaisse, crab lasagne and... the ubiquitous steak.

Hideaway Kitchen & Bar
2657 Gold Coast Highway, Broadbeach; tel: 5679 0369; http://hideawaykitchen.com.au; daily 5pm–11pm, Sat–Sun 12pm–midnight; $$-$$$
Only opened in 2016, they are putting a modern spin on Asian street food with items such as Organic locally made tofu in spicy dashi broth spring onion curls & sliced chili to start and their lamb shank curry potatoes.

Rivea Italian Dining
89 Surf Parade, Broadbeach; tel:

Modern styling at Absynthe

5538 0055; http://rivea.com.au; daily 11.30am–10pm; $$

This casual restaurant offers classic Italian dishes, from homemade pizzas and pasta to seafood.

ESPL Coffee Brewers

Soul Boardwalk, 4 Esplanade, Surfers Paradise; tel: 419 247 686; daily 6am–4pm; $

This may be the best coffee spot on the beach. In addition to delicious, well-rounded coffee, the staff are incredibly warm and friendly. There is also a good selection of freshly-baked pastries.

Etsu Izakaya

2440 Gold Coast Highway, Mermaid Beach; tel: 5526 0944; www.etsu.com. au; daily 5pm–midnight; $$

Modern Japanese izakaya-style dining at its finest. The vast menu is best considered with sharing in mind. However, if you decide to dine solo the whole menu can be ordered at the bar.

Gold Coast hinterland

St Bernards Hotel

101 Alpine Terrace, Mount Tamborine; tel: 5545 1177; www.stbernardshotel.com; noon–2pm, 6–8pm; $$

Venerable St Bernards has the ambience of a country pub. Enjoy hearty pub food, served with enough flair to keep it interesting.

Binna Burra Mountain lodge

Binna Burra Mountain Lodge, Lamington National Park; tel: 5533 3622; www. binnaburralodge.com.au; daily, hours below; $$

Enjoy the sweeping ridge-top views while choosing from a casual lunch and tea menu, including burgers, salads and scones in the Lamington Tea House. Hearty breakfasts and dinners are served in the Clifftop Dining Room.

Fraser Island

Seabelle Restaurant

Kingfisher Bay Resort, Fraser Island; tel: 4120 3333; www.kingfisherbay.com; daily 5.30–9.30pm; $$$

Seabelle Restaurant offers dishes that are inspired by traditional ingredients. Try the K'gari signature plate of chargrilled crocodile, kangaroo and emu with bunya nut pesto, bush tomato chutney, rosella and chilli plum jam.

Airlie Beach

Mangrove Jacks

Airlie Beach Hotel, The Esplanade, Airlie Beach; tel: 4964 1888; www. airliebeachhotel.com.au; daily 11.30am– 2.30pm, 5.30–9.30pm, until 10pm Fri– Sat; $$$

Mangrove Jacks is a lively beachside restaurant offering a modern Australian menu of local seafood and sumptuous steaks. There are also burgers, pizzas, and pastas.

Ochre Restaurant

Cairns

Bayleaf

Corner of Lake and Gatton Streets; tel: 4047 7955; www.bayleafrestaurant.com.au; daily 6.30–9.30am, Mon–Fri noon–2pm, nightly 6pm–late

Cairns locals flock to this Balinese Restaurant. The chefs here are all graduates of the highly-regarded Bumbu Bali Restaurant and Cooking School in Bali. The pork dishes are sublime and there's a selection of curries. Also open for breakfast.

Café China

The Reef Hotel Casino, 35-41 Wharf Street; tel: 4041 2828; www.cafechina.com.au; daily 11am–2.30pm, 5pm–9.30pm; $$

Try delicious mainly Beijing and Hong Kong dishes: specialties include salt-and-pepper mud crab, Peking duck and steamed coral trout.

Simply Italian

34 Esplanade; tel: 4050 2020; http://www.simplyitaliancairns.com.au/; daily 5pm–9.30pm, Thu–Fri from 12pm; $$

The quality and value offered by this excellent Italian restaurant makes it a winner. Pizza and pasta dishes reign supreme, with highlights listed on the daily specials board.

Fusion

5/12 Spence Street; tel 4051 1388; www.fusionartbar.com.au; Tue–Thu 3pm–10pm, Fri–Sat 11am–11pm; $-$$

A funky fusion joint in the heart of Cairns, which caters for those who like their produce fresh and organic.

Khin Khao Thai Restaurant

At Aplin and Grafton Streets; tel: 4031 8581; www.khinkhao.com.au; Mon–Fri 11am–2.30pm, 5.30–10pm, Sat–Sun 5.30–10pm; $$

The best Thai restaurant in Cairns is a popular venue with an extensive menu – such as Massaman, yellow, green and red curries – making full and fantastic use of the local seafood. Service is efficient and the prices are very reasonable, including a good-value daily lunch special.

Ochre Restaurant

1 Marlin Parade; tel: 4051 0100; www.ochrerestaurant.com.au; Mon–Sat 11.30am–9.30pm; $$$

In this multi-award-winning restaurant, creative modern Australian cuisine is offered with inventive flair that uses 40 different native ingredients to enhance dishes based on kangaroo, crocodile, beef, tropical fruit and local seafood.

Salt House

6/2 Pier Point Road; tel: 4041 7733; www.salthouse.com.au; daily 6.30am–11.30am, 12pm–3pm, and 6pm–10pm; $$

This restaurant makes the most of its prime waterfront position looking out on the Coral Sea. It comes into its own at dinner when steaks and seafood are seared on the immense wood-fired grill. There's also live music.

Tamarind

Reef Casino, 35-41 Wharf Street; tel: 4030 8897; www.reefcasino.com.au/dine/tamarind-

A prime table at Oskars on Burleigh

restaurant; daily 6.30am–10am, 6pm–10pm; $$$

Set in the Reef Casino, this award-winning Asian fusion restaurant is helmed by chef Mark Jensen. The fine dining makes the most of regional ingredients, paired with an extensive wine list and a range of cocktails. There is a daily degustation menu available.

Port Douglas

Nautilus Restaurant

17 Murphy Street; tel: 4099 5330; www. nautilus-restaurant.com.au; daily 6pm–midnight; $$$

Everybody in Port Douglas goes to the Nautilus at least once to soak up the tropical ambience of a unique outdoor dining experience.

Salsa Bar and Grill

26 Wharf Street; tel: 4099 4922; www. salsaportdouglas.com.au; daily noon–10pm; $$$

Head chef Goran Zonai puts his expertise to excellent use here, delivering a menu that explodes with flavour and creativity. Tough choice between the linguini *pepperoncino* with tableland red claw, and the kangaroo fillet.

The Mexican

43 Macrossan Street, Port Douglas; tel: 4099 4441; http://www.themexicanpd.com.au; Mon–Sat 2pm–9pm; $$

Fresh Mexican dishes that incorporate local Queensland ingredients. Using traditional Mexican spices and techniques the menu includes grilled kangaroo loin and Mayan pork tacos.

Zinc

3 / 53-61 Macrossan Street; tel: 4099 6260; www.zincportdouglas.com; daily 10am–late; $$$

A long-standing Port favourite, known locally as The Tin Shed, this edge-of-the-port restaurant specialises in local seafood, serving fantastic dishes with prawns, bugs, Barramundi and other locally-caught fish.

Daintree

Julaymba Restaurant and Gallery

Daintree Eco Lodge and Spa, 20 Daintree Road, Daintree; tel: 4777 7377; www. daintree-ecolodge.com.au; daily 8am–10am, dinner from 6.30pm; $$$

This serene restaurant overlooking a freshwater lagoon infuses indigenous fruits, nuts and berries with fine-dining. Try the seafood tapas, wok-tossed fresh king prawns, or the macadamia- and herb-crusted lamb fillet.

Mission Beach

Elandra Restaurant and Bar

23 Explorers Drive, South Mission Beach; tel: 4068 8154; www.elandraresorts.com; daily 7am–9pm; $$$

Sitting high on a cliff edge where rainforest meets the sea, enjoy modern Australian cuisine with an Asian influence, such as seared king scallops drunken chicken or a warm Asian noodle salad.

Crowds at Brisbane Powerhouse Centre for the Arts

NIGHTLIFE

Don't go looking for wall-to-wall sophistication in Queensland, particularly in the north. Nightlife in Cairns, Airlie Beach, and Mission Beach focuses largely on the backpacker party circuit, featuring themed nightclubs and barn-sized pubs with live entertainment and boozy deals. In all Australian nightclubs, bars and casinos, entry is restricted to over-18s; the young and young-looking may have to show ID.

That said, there is a healthy and growing live music scene in Queensland, which cuts across various genres. Various venues support local, national, and international acts – so keep your eye on billboards and the street press, and you may find yourself watching a band that's considered 'big' in their homeland in an intimate pub or club setting in Queensland.

For those with higher brows, Brisbane is your best bet for a bit of class. The Queensland Performing Arts Centre (www.qpac.com.au) in South Bank is the major hub for the city's cultural entertainment.

Nightlife venues and session times in Brisbane are listed in the daily *Courier-Mail*, and there are free publications such as *Rave, Time Off* and *Scene*, which can be picked up at venues and cafés. Try also www.mustdobrisbane.com.

General listings for the Cairns area can be found in Friday's *Cairns Post*.

The following is just a very small selection of what else is on offer.

Brisbane

Alfred & Constance

132 Constance St, Fortitude Valley; tel: 3252 5990; www.alfredandconstance.com.au; Mon 7am–3pm, Tue–Sat 7am–late

With three bars and a cocktail list as long as your arm, there's plenty to pour into yourself at A&C. Try a spiked Stone-fruit Superstar for starters, or sip a long glass at the Vanguard Beer Garden Bar. The White Lightning Tiki Bar is where the party will go on 'til late.

Brisbane Jazz Club

1 Annie Street, Kangaroo Point; tel: 3391 2006; www.brisbanejazzclub.com.au; Thu–Fri 6.30pm–11.30pm, Sat 3pm–11pm, Sun 11am–3pm and 5pm–10pm

Right beside the river, near the Holman Street wharf, this characterful and intimate venue hosts occasional big-name acts, Brisbane's best traditional and contemporary jazz musicians and singers, and relaxed jam sessions. Check the website for the programme and session times.

Brisbane Powerhouse Centre for the Arts

119 Lamington Street, New Farm; tel: 3358 8600; www.brisbanepowerhouse.com.au; box office Mon–Fri 9am–5pm, Sat

Brisbane at night

noon–4pm

This world-class theatre, concert hall and experimental playhouse has an ever-changing repertoire and a focus on cutting-edge performances from Australia and overseas.

Brooklyn Standard

Eagle Ln, Brisbane City; tel: 3221 1604; www.brooklynstandard.com.au; Mon–Fri 4pm–late, Sat 6pm–late

This recent winner of the 'Best Live Music Bar' award offers live music every single open night starting from 7.30pm. This basement bar offers blues, funk & soul performances along with a variety of pub food and cocktails.

Cloudland

641 Ann Street, Fortitude Valley; tel: 3852 6600; www.cloudland.tv; Tue–Sun 11am–late

From outside, the spectacular geometric facade and rough wooden door give no indication that this is a nightspot, but inside a huge atrium shelters three levels of chic bars capped by a retractable roof. There are DJs, band residencies, dancing groups and all manner of live entertainment, along with reasonably priced drinks and a restaurant.

Family

8 McLachlan Street, Fortitude Valley; tel: 3852 5000; www.thefamily.com.au; Fri–Sun 9pm–5am

Family has been voted Australia's best nightclub, with six bars, four levels, three music genres, massive sound and light technology, two huge dance floors and the capacity for 2,000 patrons. It attracts international DJs, musicians and a range of eclectic acts.

Mr & Mrs G

Eagle Street Pier 1 Eagle Street; tel: 3221 7001; www.mrandmrsg.com.au; Mon–Tue 3pm–10pm, Wed–Sun noon–late

A cool riverside cocktail bar has landed on the Eagle, one of Brisbane's premier eating streets. Named after veteran restaurateurs, Andy and Marcia Georges, it has their signature stylish look. Listen to live music here every Sunday.

Newstead Brewing Co

85 Doggett Street, Newstead; tel: 3367 0490; http://newsteadbrewing.com.au; daily 10am–midnight

Brisbane's oldest new craft brewery has a pub onsite, which stocks 12 draught beers, ales and ciders on tap - about two thirds of which are their own, the rest made of revolving selection of boutique beers from around the world. Food and take-away bottles of beer are available too.

Press Club

339 Brunswick St, Fortitude Valley; tel: 3852 5000; https://pressclub.net.au; daily 6pm–3am

Leather seating, private booths, and the occasional open-mike nights set this place apart from the rest. This boutique bar offers live music and signature

Gambling at the Reef Hotel Casino

cocktails in addition to its award winning collection of bartenders.

Story Bridge Hotel

200 Main Street, Kangaroo Point; tel: 3391 2266; www.storybridgehotel.com.au; Daily 6.30am–midnight

Situated under the famous bridge, this popular hotel has three bars and dining venues. Bands regularly play Thursday to Saturday nights, and there's live jazz on Sunday afternoons. 'Tales and Ales' is a twice-weekly storytelling and supping session where you can meet the head chef Jason Walker and learn about the beers and the brewery.

The Zoo

711 Ann Street; tel: 3854 1381; www. thezoo.com.au; Thu–Sat, times vary

Brisbane's granddaddy of live music venues champions indie acts on the whole, but also features reggae, jazz, hip hop and DJs, if they're good enough. There's no dress code, and everybody is welcome, but they do have some eccentric (and endearing) house rules: no rum is sold (too much sugar makes people hyper) and no hardcore music acts are booked (stirs up the building's ghosts).

Gold Coast

Dracula's Cabaret Restaurant

1 Hooker Boulevard, Broadbeach Waters; tel: 5563 4900; www.draculas.com.au; Tue–Sat 7pm–11pm

Part of Australia's longest-established theatre-restaurant chain, Dracula's features a dinner-cabaret show (currently 'Sin and Tonic') with magic, puppetry, musical productions and great comedy, all with classic horror themes, including a ghost train. Its blend of burlesque, theatre and comedy isn't recommended for kids under 13.

The Arts Centre Gold Coast

135 Bundall Road, Surfers Paradise; tel: 5588 4000; www.theartscentregc.com.au;

The Coast's nocturnal culture revolves around this centre. Live performances are a blend of Australian and international, old and new: Thursday is 'unplugged' in the Basement, Friday is usually comedy night, and Saturday is jazz. There's also a café, theatre and gallery.

Airlie Beach

Mama Africa Bar and Night Club

263 Shute Harbour Road, Airlie Beach; tel: 4948 0599; Tue–Sun 9pm–3am

Top DJs from all around frequent this Airlie Beach nightspot. The zebra striped dance floor is an interesting touch, as are their varied cocktails.

Cairns

Gilligans Nightclub

57-89 Grafton Street; tel: 4041 6566; www. gilligans.com.au/entertainment; daily until late

Part of a backpacker's complex, this club has three different areas for its guests including the Attic Lounge Bar

Listen to Aboriginal stories while you dine at Flames of the Forest

and a tropical lagoon pool. This is the place for late night partying in Cairns.

Pier Bar & Grill

Pierpoint Road; tel: 4031 4677; www.
pierbar.com.au; daily, 11.30am–3am

Lively bar and restaurant, perfect for relaxing on the outdoor terrace to enjoy the sea views. Live music, DJs, dancing 'til late most nights, plus a highly popular Sunday afternoon session with music and cheap pizza.

Pullman Reef Hotel Casino

35–41 Wharf Street; tel: 4030 8888; www.
reefcasino.com.au; daily, times vary

The casino has more than 500 gaming machines and more than 40 tables, as well as restaurants, bars and various kinds of live entertainment, including the Velvet Underground nightclub.

The Cotton Club

24 Shields Street; tel: 4041 1400; www.
thecottonclubcairns.com.au; daily
11.30am–3am

This is a restaurant during the day and an upscale and intimate cocktail bar and dance venue in the evenings.

The Woolshed

22-24 Shields Street, City Place; tel: 4031
6304; www.thewoolshed.com.au; daily
9pm–3am

Events and parties kick off every night of the week here, almost all of them involving the flashing of flesh to greater or lesser degrees. Open late and loud.

Port Douglas

Flames of the Forest

29 Barrier St; Tel: 4099 3966; www.
flamesoftheforest.com.au; Tue, Thu–Sat
7.30–10.30pm

Dine in the rainforest and listen to Aboriginal stories: guests are picked up from their hotels from 6pm and transported to the Mowbray Valley, where flames light a path to a clearing and candles flicker beside a stream. More candles illuminate tables, immaculately set. It's *Lord of the Rings meets Alice in Wonderland*, an original and magical experience.

The Ironbar

5 Macrossan Street; tel: 4099 4776; www.
ironbarportdouglas.com.au; daily 11am–late

A seven nights a week venue that has been going forever, the Ironbar offers everything from cane toad racing through to live music. It's open until 2am most nights.

Karnak Playhouse

Upper Whyanbeel Road, Miallo; tel: 4098
8111; www.karnakplayhouse.com.au; evening
performances May–Dec Wed and Sat.

Karnak is a little out of town, but well worth the trip, and there are bus connections from Port Douglas for performances. A range of plays is presented in a magnificent rainforest amphitheatre, which seats 500. It's also open daily during the day for light lunches, made from organic produce grown on-site, and for afternoon tea.

A–Z

A

Age restrictions

By law, to drink alcohol, smoke tobacco or get a tattoo in Queensland you must be 18 or over. Drivers in Queensland must be 17 years of age to obtain a provisional driving licence; visitors under 21 years of age typically will not be able to hire rental cars, and those under 25 will pay a premium.

The age of consent is 16.

B

Budgeting

Accommodation. A bed at a backpacker hostel can be as little as A$25 a night, and a room in a three-star hotel is usually around A$100. A room in a four- or five-star hotel can start as low as A$200, although internet and low-season deals can halve even this tariff.

Airport taxi. A taxi from Brisbane Airport to central Brisbane will cost around A$50. From Cairns Airport to central Cairns costs about A$25. Train and/or bus options are also available.

Buses and ferries. A single (2-hour) ticket that allows travel on Brisbane's buses, trains and ferries within one zone costs around A$4.80. If you're planning on being in the city for some time, consider getting a Go-Card, which will save

you roughly 30 percent of what you'll pay if you continue using paper tickets.

Car rental. Renting a small car costs from A$45 per day; a 4WD will cost A$100-150 per day. Petrol (gasoline) costs around A$1.60 per litre.

Dive courses. Prices range from A$550–900 for courses that include open-water diving on day trips; more expensive courses include on-board accommodation and meals.

Restaurants. A main course in a budget restaurant costs about A$20, A$25-40 at a moderate restaurant, and A$40–50 at an expensive restaurant. A bottle of Australian wine from a bottle shop (liquor store) starts at about A$10; the same bottle in a restaurant is likely to cost A$25, hence the popularity of BYO (Bring Your Own) restaurants. A glass of house wine averages around A$8-10. A 'pot' of full-strength draught beer (see page 19) costs from A$5.50, and a cup of espresso coffee or tea is a bit cheaper (around A$3.50).

C

Children

Australia is a great place to travel with kids, and Queensland is particularly well suited to young families. Coastal Queensland is one big playground, from theme parks on the Gold Coast to koala cuddling at Australia Zoo and Cairns

Hussar snapper, Great Barrier Reef

Tropical Zoo, to snorkelling on a coral reef. The Queensland Museum and Wheel of Brisbane on Brisbane's South Bank are sure to please, and at Tjapukai Aboriginal Cultural Park in Cairns the daily shows include an evening of corroboree around a fire. Child-concession admission usually applies to children 12 years and under, but it can be as old as 16. Check the *Yellow Pages* directory for professional baby-sitting services.

Clothing

In subtropical Brisbane, dress is informal and casual, though some hotels, restaurants and clubs will require a jacket and tie in the evening. Lightweight clothing is suitable year-round, but bring something warm in case the temperature drops at night, especially in autumn and winter. In Cairns' tropical climate, dress is always informal, with very few restaurants and clubs requiring a jacket and tie. Lightweight clothing is suitable all year round, but again bring something warm for cool winter nights in the highlands. To protect yourself against sunstroke and sunburn, you should wear sunscreen, a broad-brimmed hat, good sunglasses and a shirt with collar and sleeves. Bring swimwear and rash vests (tightfitting, quick drying tops) for the beach.

Crime and safety

Brisbane, Cairns, and the Gold Coast are fairly safe, but do not leave valuables unattended or in parked cars. Avoid dark, empty spaces and public toilets at night,

and be aware of the potential of alcohol-fuelled violence around nightclubs. If visiting the Gold Coast, particularly the Sunshine Coast, avoid, if at all possible, the 'schoolies' season from the end of November to mid-December, when huge numbers of teenagers descend on the place and basically get loaded. It's more annoying than dangerous – but it can certainly negatively affect your experience. The police are helpful and competent.

Customs

Non-dutiable allowances are 25g of tobacco products and 2,250ml (a quart) of beer, wine or spirits, and other dutiable goods to the total value of A$900, plus personal clothing, footwear and toiletries. Up to A$450-worth of dutiable goods, not including alcohol or tobacco, are allowed in the baggage of children under 18. Visit www.customs.gov.au for further information.

Strict quarantine regulations forbid the importation of foods, plants, animals and their by-products. Heavy jail penalties apply to the smuggling of drugs of any kind. Visitors are allowed to carry up to four weeks' supply of prescribed medications, but for larger supplies you should carry a doctor's certificate for customs purposes.

Disabled travellers

A useful booklet, *Accessible Queensland*, and information on other support

Looking out over Brisbane

services (available Mon–Fri) can be obtained from the Disability Information Awareness Line (DIAL), tel: 3224 8444 in Brisbane, or toll-free outside Brisbane on 1800 177 120 (international callers should dial +61 7 3224 8444).

E

Electricity

Electrical power is 240/250v AC, 50Hz Universal. Most hotels also have outlets for 110v (shavers only). Adaptors for Australian power outlets are readily available at the airport and in shops and hotels.

Embassies and consulates

The following are the closest contacts for travellers needing assistance when in Queensland.

British Consular Agency, Level 9 Waterfront Place, 100 Eagle Street, Brisbane; tel: 3223 3200; http://ukinaustralia.fco.gov.uk

Canadian Consulate General, Level 5, 6/111 Harrington Street, Sydney; tel: 02 9364 3000; recorded information: 02 9364 3050; www.international.gc.ca

Consulate General of Ireland, Level 26, 1 Market Street, Sydney; tel: 02 9264 9635; www.irishconsulatesydney.net

US Consulate General, MLC Centre, Level 10, 19–29 Martin Place, Sydney; tel: 02 9373 9200; after-hours emergencies, tel: 02 4422 2201; https://au.usembassy.gov

Emergencies

In an emergency, dial 000 for police, fire or ambulance services.

G

Green issues

Queenslanders take environmental issues seriously, particularly in the heavily populated coastal regions. The recent decision by the Federal Australian Government to approve increased mining and industrial activity (including sea floor dredging and the dumping of silt) to take place in the World Heritage–listed Area of the Great Barrier Reef has caused a large amount of disquiet among local operators and environmentalists and the concerned public. For more information on this and other threats to the health of the Great Barrier Reef from mining activity, coral bleaching, and other manmade issues, see www.greatbarrierreef.com.au For additional information on how climate change threatens the Great Barrier Reef, see www.gbrmpa.gov.au/corp_site/key_issues/climate_change. Recycling of glass, paper, aluminium and certain plastics is widespread; look for recycling bins with yellow lids.

Air travel produces a huge amount of carbon dioxide and is a significant contributor to global warming. If you would like to offset the damage caused to the environment by your flight, a number of

Eumundi art gallery

organisations can do this for you, using online 'carbon calculators', which tell you how much you need to donate. In the UK travellers can visit www.climate care.org or www.carbonneutral.com; in the US log on to www.climatefriendly. com or www.sustainabletravelinterna tional.org.

H

Health

Australia has excellent medical services. For medical attention out of working hours go to the casualty department of a major hospital or, if the matter is less urgent, visit one of the medical clinics in the major towns and tourist centres. Look under 'Medical Centres' or 'Medical Practitioners' in the *Yellow Pages*, or ask at your hotel.

Healthcare and insurance

Citizens of countries with which Australia has a reciprocal agreement (UK, Ireland, Finland, Norway, Sweden, Malta, Netherlands, New Zealand, Belgium, Italy, and Slovenia) are allowed restricted access to government Medicare service; this covers free care as a patient in hospital and subsidised medicines. It does not cover dental care, ambulance costs or emergency evacuation to your home country, so you are advised to take out your own travel insurance. Visitors from other countries should have private insurance to cover all medical care. See www.health.gov.au for details.

Inoculations

No vaccinations are necessary for entry into Australia unless you have visited an area (including parts of South America and Africa) infected by yellow fever, cholera or typhoid in the previous 14 days.

Natural health hazards

The biggest danger for travellers in Australia is the sun. Even on mild, cloudy days it has the potential to burn. Wear a broad-brimmed hat and, if you are planning on being out for a while, a long-sleeved shirt made from a light fabric. Wear SPF 30+ sunblock at all times, even under a hat.

Apart from jellyfish (see page 28), the main danger in north Queensland's coastal waters are saltwater (or estuarine) crocodiles. Do not enter waters where crocodile warning signs are posted, always ask for local advice, and if in doubt do not venture in. Some species of shark do pose a potential risk, albeit not as big as most people's fears lead them to believe. To be extra cautious, avoid swimming in murky water, with dogs or close to where pipes pump water or waste out to sea. Swimming in some areas – around the coast of Fraser Island for example – is actively discouraged. Listen to the advice of locals and always pay attention to warning signs on beaches. Scuba diving is very safe and takes place in extremely controlled conditions.

Pharmacies and hospitals

'Chemist shops' are a great place to go for advice on minor ailments such as

bites, scratches and stomach trouble. They also stock a wide range of useful products such as sunblock, nappies (diapers) and non-prescription drugs. If you have a prescription from your doctor, and you want to take it to a pharmacist in Australia, you will need to have it endorsed by a local medical practitioner.

Hours and holidays

Business hours

Core business hours are generally Mon–Thu 9am–5.30pm, Fri until 9pm in the cities, Sat 9am–1pm. However, retailers tend to follow demand, and hours vary widely, with most shops in tourist precincts open on Saturday afternoon and Sunday.

Public holidays

Banks, post offices, government and private offices close on the following holidays:

New Year's Day (1 Jan)
Australia Day (26 Jan)
Good Friday (date variable)
Easter Monday (date variable)
Anzac Day (25 April)
Labour Day (First Monday in May)
Queen's Birthday (2nd Monday in June)
Christmas Day (25 Dec)
Boxing Day (26 Dec)

Internet facilities

Internet cafés, while no longer as prolific they were, are still prevalent, and travellers to Australia should have no trouble finding internet access in major cities and tourist locations. Many standard cafés, pubs and restaurants offer free Wi-Fi (be sure to buy something at least once an hour). Most hotels and hostels now have facilities for people travelling with their own laptops – although some persist in charging per minute or hour – and local libraries fill the gap in communities where there is no commercial internet facility.

Left luggage

At Brisbane Airport there are left-luggage facilities in the international terminal and outside the Qantas and Virgin terminals at the domestic terminal. Cairns Airport has a baggage-storage facility (best to email them at park@cairnsairport.com.au). There are lockers for luggage on all levels of Brisbane's Transit Centre at Roma Street. To check the facilities available at other Queensland train stations, see www.queenslandrailtravel.com.au.

LGBTQ travellers

Queensland may not have quite the same gay sub-culture that you would find in Sydney, but there is a thriving LGBTQ community in the state's capital, and Noosa is a favoured spot to wind down after the Sydney Gay Mardi Gras in March.

To find the rainbow edge to Brisbane's nightlife, try The Wickham Hotel

Always heed danger signs at the beach

(www.thewickham.com.au) in Fortitude Valley or Spring Hill's Sportsman Hotel (www.sportsmanhotel.com.au), the oldest gay bar in town. Brisbane's Pride Festival (https://brisbanepride.org.au) is held each June. The highlight of the month-long festival is generally a parade and fair day.

Check out the gay press for further information; *Queensland Pride* is a free monthly newspaper, and *Q News* is a free fortnightly newspaper; both are based in Brisbane. Gay and Lesbian Tourism Australia (www.galta.com.au) promotes gay-friendly tourism operators.

Lost property

Report the loss or theft of valuables to the police immediately, as most insurance policies insist on a police report. In Brisbane, lost property found at a Citytrain station is held for three days at that particular station before being forwarded to Roma Street Station (tel: 3238 4500. For anything left on Brisbane's ferries, tel: 3229 7778, daily 9am–5pm.

To locate property left on a Brisbane bus, contact the Brisbane City Council call centre, tel: 3403 8888.

M

Maps

Officially accredited Visitor Information Centres, indicated by the yellow 'i' against a blue background, give away useful maps of their areas. The Queensland Holidays website carries a map of Queensland showing the locations of the Visitor Centres. Visit the RACQ Travel Centres (www.racq.com.au) for touring maps. They can also be mailed overseas to international visitors.

Media

Print and online media

Brisbane's daily newspaper is the *Courier-Mail* (www.couriermail.com.au), a lively tabloid published Monday to Saturday. On Sunday the major Brisbane newspaper is the *Sunday Mail*. Both are part of the News Corporation stable. In Cairns the local daily is the *Cairns Post* (www.cairnspost.com.au).

Australia has two national papers, the *Australian* (www.theaustralian.com.au) and the *Australian Financial Review* (www.afr.com). In 2013, the British paper *The Guardian* launched an Australian version of the paper online: www.theguardian.com/au. Foreign-language newspapers and magazines are available at newsagents in Brisbane, the airport and major tourist districts.

Radio and television

The Australian Broadcasting Commission (ABC) runs national television channels as well as an extensive network of radio stations. ABC television offers excellent news and current affairs, as well as local and imported drama, comedy, sports and cultural programmes. The commercial TV sta-

Cairns marina

tions, Channels 7, 9 and 10, offer news, drama, soaps, infotainment, travel shows and, between them, coverage of most of the major international sporting events. Foxtel (www.foxtel.com.au) is the major pay television company in the country, operating cable, direct broadcast satellite television and IPTV services. Many hotels provide access to a large number of cable television stations.

Radio stations include Triple J (107.7 FM in Brisbane and 107.5 in Cairns, or listen online from anywhere www.abc.net.au/triplej), rock and comment for the twentysomethings; Classic FM (106.1 FM in Brisbane and 105.9 FM, www.abc.net.au/classic), continuous classical music; and Radio National (792 AM and 105.1 FM in Cairns, www.abc.net.au/radionational), excellent national news and events coverage. Commercial radio stations include Triple M FM (104.7 in Brisbane, www.triplem.com.au/brisbane) for popular local and international rock, and Nova 1069 for contemporary music (106.9 FM, www.novafm.com.au/station/nova1069).

Of particular interest to overseas travellers is Australia's ethnic/multicultural broadcaster, SBS (www.sbs.com.au). The organisation's excellent television channel offers many foreign-language films and documentaries, and Australia's best coverage of world news. SBS Radio (93.3 FM in Brisbane, www.sbs.com.au/radio) offers programmes in a variety of languages.

Money

The four major banks in Australia are ANZ, Commonwealth, National Australia and Westpac. There's also the Bank of Queensland (www.boq.com.au). Trading hours are generally Mon–Thu 9am–4pm and Fri 9am–5pm.

Cash machines

Most bank branches have automatic teller machines (ATMs) that are networked with Cirrus, Maestro, and other networks, allowing you to access funds from overseas accounts. Many will charge you to withdraw cash.

Credit cards

Most establishments display a list of the credit cards they will accept, usually including MasterCard and Visa, and less so Amex, Diners Club and JCB.

Currency

Australia's currency is the dollar (A$), which is divided into 100 cents. The polymer (plastic) notes come in denominations of 5, 10, 20, 50 and 100 dollars, each of which has a distinctly different colour. Coins come in denominations of 5, 10, 20 and 50 cents (silver-coloured), and one and two dollars (bronze-coloured). The one-dollar coin is, confusingly, larger than the two. There are no one- or two-cent coins, so shopkeepers round up change to the nearest five cents.

The old Cairns Post building

Taxes

The Australian government collects a 10 percent goods and services tax (GST) on virtually all retail sales. Under a 'tourist refund scheme', the GST on goods valued at over A$300, bought from the same shop within the previous 30 days and carried as hand luggage, can be recovered upon leaving the country at a Tourist Refund Scheme (TRS) booth located beyond customs at the airport; you must have retained the tax invoice. For more details, go here: http://www.customs.gov.au/site/page4646.asp.

Tipping

Tipping is not customary even for taxi drivers and restaurant staff, but it is not unusual to reward good service with a gratuity of between 10 and 15 percent of the bill. Hotel staff do not solicit or expect tips, but certainly will not be offended by one.

Travellers' cheques

It is becoming increasingly uncommon for people to use travellers' cheques, but all well-known brands can usually be exchanged at banks, five-star hotels and exchange bureaux.

P

Police

In an emergency call 000. At other times call the local police station, which can be located on www.police.qld.gov.au

Post

Australian Post (http://auspost.com.au) offices are open Mon–Fri 9am–5pm; some post shops are also open Sat 9am–noon. The Brisbane GPO (261 Queen Street) is open Mon–Fri 7am–6pm. One of the main post offices in Cairns is at 38 Sheridan Street (Mon–Fri 8.30am–5.30pm). Post offices will hold properly addressed mail for visitors and sell stamps, standard and Express Post envelopes and packaging. Post boxes are red (standard mail) or yellow (Express Post).

The cost of overseas mail depends on the weight and size of the package. To send a postcard to Europe or the USA costs A$3. A letter up to 50g in weight will also cost A$3.

S

Smoking

In Queensland it is illegal to smoke inside restaurants, bars and clubs, including commercial outdoor eating or drinking areas, at patrolled beaches, and major sports stadiums. Additionally, it is illegal to smoke in a car carrying children under the age of 16.

T

Telephones

The international code for Australia is 61 and the area code for Queensland is 07.

Within Queensland, you do not need to dial this code.

To call from Australia, dial 0011 + country code + area code (drop the first 0) + number. The country code for Canada and the US is 1, Ireland is 353 and the UK is 44.

There are plenty of public telephones and most take phone cards. All Australian coins can be used in payphones, though many public phones only use phone cards, which can be bought in general stores, post offices and newsagents. For eight-figure numbers, you dial the 07 area code only if you're calling from outside Queensland. For Directory Assistance, dial 1223.

Mobile (cell) phones

The GSM 900 mobile phone system network in Australia is compatible with systems everywhere except Japan and the Americas. To use your mobile here for a short term you should buy an Australian SIM card with prepaid calls. Providers include Telstra (www.telstra.com.au), Optus (www.optus.com.au), Vodaphone (www.vodafone.com.au) and Virgin Mobile (www.virginmobile.com.au).

Time zones

Queensland operates on Australian Eastern Standard Time (Greenwich Mean Time plus 10 hours). Daylight saving is not observed in Queensland, but does apply, from different dates, in the other states across three time zones, giving, at worst, up to six differing times across the country.

Tourist information

Before you leave home, visit the Tourism Australia website: www.australia.com. Queensland is well served by organisations designed to help visitors. In addition to information centres, the following websites will answer almost any questions that you might have: www.experiencequeensland.com; www.queenslandholidays.com.au

The main tourist information centres in Queensland are:

Brisbane

Corner Albert and Queen streets; tel: 3006 6290; www.visitbrisbane.com.au, and the Southern Queensland Visitors Information Centre, Level 2, Brisbane International Airport; tel: 3406 3190; www.southernqueensland.com.au

Cairns

Corner of Aplin Street and the Esplanade; tel: 4047 9125; www.cairnstouristinformation.com.au

Gold Coast

2 Cavill Avenue, Surfers Paradise; tel: 1300 309 440; www.visitgoldcoast.com

Mission Beach

55 Porters Promenade; tel: 4068 7099; www.missionbeachtourism.com

Noosa

61 Hastings Street, Noosa Heads; tel: 5430 5000; www.visitnoosa.com.au

Whitsunday Coast

Tourism Whitsundays; Bruce Highway; tel: 4945 3967; www.tourismwhitsundays.com.au/visitor-information

Qantas is Australia's national airline

Transport

Airports

Many international airlines provide regular links between Brisbane Airport (www.bne. com.au) and Europe, the US and Asian and Pacific nations. Frequent Qantas and Virgin Blue domestic services fly to Brisbane and Coolangatta (www.goldcoastairport. com.au) from Sydney, Melbourne, Canberra and other state capitals.

Brisbane Airport's adjacent international and domestic terminals are connected by shuttle bus. Few hotels provide regular courtesy coach transfers, but some will do so on request. Cabs to the city are expensive. However, a combination of comfortable, regular Airport Commuter coaches and a fast shuttle train takes you to and from the central city terminal at Roma Street with shuttles from there to many of the downtown hotels. Translink (tel: 13 12 30; www.translink.com.au) can provide all the travel information you need. A cab ride to the central business district costs about A$50.

Cairns Airport (www.cairnsairport.com) has regular air links to Asia and the Pacific as well as to Brisbane, Sydney and Melbourne. The airport is 8km (5 miles) from central Cairns. Many hotels provide coach transfers, or Sun Palm's Express Coaches (tel: 4087 1191; http://sunpalmtransport. com.au) cost A$15 to Cairns hotels. Airport Connection (tel: 4049 2244; www.tnqshuttle.com) services Port Douglas, the Northern Beaches, and Palm Cove.

Public transport

Translink (tel: 13 12 30; www.translink. com.au) is responsible for public transport by bus, train and ferry transportation throughout the region.

Rail and long-distance bus

Brisbane's main rail terminal is the Transit Centre in Roma Street, a short taxi ride to/from most Brisbane hotels. Fast trains travel to Robina on the Gold Coast at half-hour intervals most of the day, every hour during less busy times. The *Spirit of Queensland* rail service (five times weekly) along the coast from Brisbane to Cairns takes about 24 hours. Contact Queensland Rail's Traveltrain Holidays (tel: 1300 132 722; www.queenslandrail travel.com.au).

Coaches to Surfers Paradise, Southport and other Coast destinations are provided by Surfside Buslines (www.surf side.com.au). Both Greyhound Australia (www.greyhound.com.au) and Premier Motor Service (www.premierms.com.au) service the major resort towns along the East Coast between Brisbane and Cairns; the direct journey between the two cities takes 29 hours. Check out the Brisbane <> Cairns Hop On, Hop Off ticket with Greyhound. Just pick your direction and enjoy the amazing sights.

Taxis

Taxis showing a light can be flagged down from the kerb. Rates per km are around A$2, plus an A$4-6 initial charge. A small phone booking fee is charged if

Brisbane's ANZAC square

you call a cab, and most cabs take credit cards. Taxis normally carry only four passengers, but maxi-cabs, which take six to 10 passengers, are available on request for an additional surcharge. Smoking is banned in all cabs, and the passenger may be fined if not wearing a seatbelt. To book a cab (just about anywhere in Australia) call tel: 131 008.

Car rental

International car-hire companies offer good discounts on pre-booked hires, with the option to return the vehicle to another major centre at no extra charge. The minimum age for hiring a car is 21, but drivers under 25 pay a surcharge. A national driving licence is acceptable if it is written in English; otherwise you should obtain an international driver's licence. If your picture ID is not on the licence, you may have to produce your passport. Insurance on conventional rental cars is invalid on unsealed (dirt) roads, but most hire companies insure 4WD vehicles for any road that is shown on a map. Cover for single-vehicle accidents is subject to a high excess payment. Major international car-rental firms include:

Avis (tel: 1300 137 498; www.avis.com. au)

Budget (tel: 1300 362 848; www.budget. com.au)

Europcar (tel: 1300 131 390; www. europcar.com.au)

Hertz (tel: 13 30 39; www.hertz.com.au)

Thrifty (tel: 1300 367 227; www.thrifty. com.au).

Driving

Traffic drives on the left in Australia, so you usually give way to the right and road signs usually match international rules. There is a 0.05 percent blood alcohol limit for drivers, which is widely enforced by the practice of random breath tests. Police also conduct random drug tests – both involve stopping entire lanes of traffic, or even whole roads.

Off-road driving

When driving on sand it is always advisable to carry a 'snatch strap' in the event of getting bogged in loose sand. Check with your 4WD hire company that you have one in your vehicle. Also consult them for the correct tyre pressure for your vehicle. Queensland boasts the full podium when it comes to big sand islands: Fraser Island, the world's biggest, North Stradbroke, the second biggest, and Moreton Island, which takes bronze. To drive on any of these islands you must get a Vehicle Access Permit from the Department of Parks, Recreation, Sport and Racing (NPRSR), go here for more information: http://nprsr.qld.gov.au/recreation-areas/vehicle_access_permit_fees.html. Lowering pressure in your tyres makes driving on sand safer and easier. However, do not forget to re-inflate your tyres once again when driving on bitumen. Also note that speed limits are signposted and enforced.

Cycling over Goodwill Bridge in Brisbane

Tours

If you don't fancy driving your own 4WD, take a guided day tour. Many operators offer these from Brisbane including Sunrover Expeditions (tel: 3203 4241; www.sunrover.com.au). Alternatively, take the Tangalooma Launch and book a Tangalooma Resort tour (tel: 3637 2000; www.tangalooma.com).

You can also take a guided tour of Fraser Island from Brisbane and Hervey Bay; operators include Cool Dingo Tours (www.cooldingotour.com), Sunrover Expeditions (www.sunrover.com.au) and Bushwacker Ecotours (www.bushwacker-ecotours.com.au). Another option is to join one of the resort's ranger-guided day tours from Kingfisher Bay Resort.

V

Visas and passports

Your passport must be valid for at least six months from your date of arrival into Australia. All non-Australian citizens need a valid visa to enter Australia, with the exception of New Zealand citizens travelling on New Zealand passports, who are issued with a visa on arrival in Australia. Visas are available from Australian visa offices such as Australian embassies, high commissions and consulates, and from travel agents and airlines in some countries.

The **Electronic Transfer Authority** (ETA) enables visitors to obtain a visa on the spot from their travel agent or airline office. The system is in place for a number of countries, including the US and Canada. ETA visas are generally valid over a 12-month period; single stays must not exceed three months, but return visits within the 12-month period are allowed. ETAs are issued free, or you can purchase one online for A\$20 from www.eta.immi.gov.au.

Most EU citizens are eligible for an **eVisitor** visa, which is free and can be obtained online. **Tourist visas** are available for continuous stays longer than three months, but must be obtained from an Australian visa office, such as an embassy or consulate. A\$20 fee applies. Those travelling on any kind of tourist visa are not permitted to work while in Australia.

Working Holiday Visas are obtainable for citizens of some countries (including the United Kingdom, Canada, France, Germany, the Netherlands and Ireland) who are between the ages of 18 and 30 (Canadian and Irish citizens can be up to 35).

The concept behind the visa is to encourage cultural exchange and closer ties between Australia and eligible countries. People must be outside Australia when they apply for their first Working Holiday visa and when the visa is decided. The initial period of the visa is 12 months, but in certain circumstance (such as if the visa holder spends a period working in a rural area where there is a labour shortage) it can be extended for a further year. For more information, visit the website: www.immi.gov.au/Visas/Pages/417.aspx.

Steve Irwin, the Crocodile Hunter

BOOKS AND FILM

Queensland may not enjoy a literary or cinematic tradition quite as rich as some of its sibling states, but the immense landscapes, dramatic conditions and eccentric population of the East Coast has produced a few great actors – among them Margot Robbie, Geoffrey Rush, and Aboriginal star Deborah Mailman – and inspired notable writers and filmmakers.

Film

One of Australia's most popular screen characters ever was based on a true-blue Queensland icon: the anemonefish or the clown fish. *Finding Nemo* (2003) was a colossal global hit, introducing several generations of kids to the underwater cast and crew of the Great Barrier Reef and, somewhat ironically, causing a massive spike in number of clown fish being kept in captivity around the world. In 2016, the world finally got to watch the long-awaited sequel, *Finding Dory*.

Steve Irwin's *The Crocodile Hunter: Collision Course* (2002) may have proved that acting wasn't the great man's strong suit, but the film was an unlikely international success.

It's worth mentioning that Paul Hogan's beloved *Crocodile Dundee* (1986) did all his best work in Queensland's tropics, before hopping off to New York to demonstrate what a real knife looks like. The pub that appears in the film is the Walkabout Creek Hotel in McKinlay.

Queensland's more critically acclaimed big screen appearances include a starring role in *The Proposition* (2005), a brutally gritty Australian western written by the dark pen of Nick Cave and featuring the acting talents of British heavyweights Ray Winstone, John Hurt and Emily Watson, along with local luminaries Guy Pearce, Noah Taylor, David Wenham and Aboriginal actor David Gulpilil. Set in the 1880s, the film was shot on location in the blistering heat of Winton, deep in the Queensland outback.

This harsh terrain inspired Queenslander George Miller, writer and director of the cult *Mad Max* films (1979–1981), to create his dystopian world and the anti-hero that launched the career of Mel Gibson (who famously scored the role after auditioning with a battered face, having been in a drunken brawl the night before).

The 21st century brought quite a few superhero and fantasy films to Queensland. *The Chronicles of Narnia: the Voyage of the Dawn Tender*, *Thor: Ragnarok*, and *Aquaman* were all partially shot and located here.

Miller, from Chinchilla in the Darling Ranges of the Gold Coast's hinterland, later wrote the animation hit *Happy Feet* (2006), a kids' film with an environmental sub-message about a group of singing-and-dancing emperor penguins, which starred the voices of numerous Australians (including Hugh Jackman and Steve

Clown fish

Peter Carey

Irwin, who died during production and whose memory the film is dedicated to).

Other notable films wholly or partially shot in Queensland include the rom-com **Muriel's Wedding** (1994) starring Australians Toni Collette and Rachel Griffiths, which features scenes shot in Coolangatta, the Gold Coast, Surfers Paradise and Hamilton Island – and the crime comedy **Gettin' Square** (2004), with Sam Worthington, David Wenham, Gary Sweet and British actor Timothy Spall.

And then there's the shark-based horror genre, to which Queensland has contributed two films – **Open Water** (2003) and **The Reef** (2010) – both loosely based on true stories, the latter a shipwreck yarn and the first a tale about an American couple who get left behind by their boat while on a scuba-diving trip to the Great Barrier Reef.

Arguably the greatest work completed with cameras in Queensland, though, was the three-part series **The Great Barrier Reef** (screened in 2012), filmed by the BBC and narrated by marine biologist Monty Halls.

Books

Brisbane-based writer Nick Earls has been likened to British pop-culture scribe Nick Hornby. Earls writes poignant and funny fictional novels about everyday life. His award-winning books include **Zigzag Street** and the young-adult novel, **48 Shades of Brown**.

British-born but Queensland raised, John Birmingham initially found fame with **He Died With A Felafel In His Hand** and **The Tasmanian Babes Fiasco**. The first is a tragic-funny account of life in shared accommodation around Australia, based on Birmingham's own experiences, which was later turned into a film. *The Tasmanian Babes Fiasco* was re-interpreted as a play by 36 unemployed actors, who turned it into Australian's longest-running stage play.

Birmingham has since explored different genres, with techno thriller **Weapons of Choice**, his **Axis of Time** trilogy and a series – **Without Warning**, **After America** and **Angels of Vengeance** – an imaginative look at the world after American society has been destroyed by an apocalyptic energy field.

One of Australia's most highly regarded authors is Peter Carey – a two-time winner of the Booker prize (for **Oscar and Lucinda** and **True History of the Kelly Gang**). While Queensland can't claim Carey, he did write his first published novel **Bliss** (1981) while living in an alternative community called Starlight in Yandina, north of Brisbane – an experience that clearly influences the narrative.

Other notable writers to emerge from Queensland include Brisbane-born David Malouf, whose epic **The Great World** (1990) – which recounts the experiences of two Australians through the turmoil of the World Wars – saw him win the Commonwealth Writers' Prize and the French Prix Femina Étranger. He was also shortlisted for the Booker Prize for his novel **Remembering Babylon**.

ABOUT THIS BOOK

This *Explore Guide* has been produced by the editors of Insight Guides, whose books have set the standard for visual travel guides since 1970. With top-quality photography and authoritative recommendations, these guidebooks bring you the very best routes and itineraries in the world's most exciting destinations.

BEST ROUTES

The routes in the book provide something to suit all budgets, tastes and trip lengths. As well as covering the destination's many classic attractions, the itineraries track lesser-known sights, and there are also excursions for those who want to extend their visit outside the city. The routes embrace a range of interests, so whether you are an art fan, a gourmet, a history buff or have kids to entertain, you will find an option to suit. We recommend reading the whole of a route before setting out. This should help you to familiarise yourself with it and enable you to plan where to stop for refreshments – options are shown in the 'Food and Drink' box at the end of each tour. For our pick of the tours by theme, consult Recommended Routes for… (see pages 6–7).

INTRODUCTION

The routes are set in context by this introductory section, giving an overview of the destination to set the scene, plus background information on food and drink, shopping and more, while a history timeline highlights the key events over the centuries.

DIRECTORY

Also supporting the routes is a Directory chapter, with a clearly organised A–Z of practical information, our pick of where to stay while you are there and select restaurant listings; these eateries complement the more low-key cafés and restaurants that feature within the routes and are intended to offer a wider choice for evening dining. Also included here are some nightlife listings and our recommendations for books and films about the destination.

ABOUT THE AUTHORS

Patrick Kinsella a freelance journalist and editor, has the good fortune to be a dual citizen of Australia and the UK, enabling him to enjoy the delights of both and experience their vastly contrasting wonders with new eyes each time he swaps hemisphere. He spent much of the last decade mountain biking across the Tablelands behind Cairns and Port Douglas, hiking across the Hinterland behind the Gold Coast, diving along the Great Barrier Reef, sipping cold beers on beaches and ejoying great coffee in Brisbane. This book builds on original content by Lindsay Brown, a former marine biologist who divides his time between Australia and South Asia, and Cathy Finch, a Queensland-based writer and photographer.

CONTACT THE EDITORS

We hope you find this Explore Guide useful, interesting and a pleasure to read. If you have any questions or feedback on the text, pictures or maps, please do let us know. If you have noticed any errors or outdated facts, or have suggestions for places to include on the routes, please drop us an email at hello@insightguides.com. Thanks!

CREDITS

Explore Queensland
Editor: Tatiana Wilde
Author: Patrick Kinsella
Head of DTP and Pre-Press: Rebeka Davies
Update Production: Apa Digital
Managing Editor: Carine Tracanelli
Picture Editor: Tom Smyth
Cartography: original cartography Phoenix Mapping, updated by Carte
Photo credits: Alamy 19L, 22, 42/43, 54/55; AWL Images 86; Brisbane Powerhouse 120; Cairns Regional Gallery 6BC, 74; Cairns Tropical Zoo 85L; Cairns Wildlife Dome 76; CITY publicity 117; Coffee Works Experience 93L; Coral Princess Cruises 28, 30/31, 34ML; Coral Sea Resort 111; Dreamstime 43L, 56, 72, 122, 132/133, 136/137; E'cco Bistro 115; Flames of the Forest 123; Fotolia 97; Getty Images 70/71; iStockphoto 1, 6TL, 7MR, 8/9T, 14, 17, 36, 41L, 51, 52/53, 66, 96, 100MC, 105, 116, 124/125; Jerry Dennis/Apa Publications 18/19; John Gollings 4ML; Jungle Surfing 89; Kingfisher Bay Resort 65; Kuranda Scenic Railway 80, 81; Kuranda Skyrail 78; Mark Pokorny/Queensland Folk Federation Inc 23; Mary Evans Picture Library 32; Moviestore Collection/Rex 136; Murray Fredericks Photography 7T, 112/113, 114; O'Reilly's Guesthouse 62, 63L; Ochre Restaurant 118; Oskars Restaurant 34MR, 119; Palazzo Versace 110; Peter Stuckings/Apa Publications 4MC, 4MR, 4MR, 7MR, 8ML, 8MC, 8MR, 10, 11, 13L, 12/13, 15L, 14/15, 18, 20, 21, 24, 34MC, 34MR, 34ML, 34MC, 34/35T, 36/37, 37L, 38, 39L, 38/39, 40, 40/41, 42, 44, 45, 50, 52, 53L, 58, 59L, 58/59, 60, 61L, 60/61, 62/63, 64, 73, 74/75, 75L, 77L, 79, 84, 84/85, 88, 90, 91, 92, 92/93, 94/95, 100ML, 100MR, 100ML, 100/101T, 106/107, 108, 108/109, 121, 126, 127, 128/129, 130, 131, 134, 135; Pictures Colour Library 87; Press Association Images 137L; Quicksilver and Great Adventures 30, 31L; Raging Thunder 25L; Shutterstock 4/5T, 66/67, 76/77; Spirit of Freedom 28/29, 29L; Stamford Hotels and Resorts 102, 103; State Library of Queensland 33; Tangalooma Island Resort 6MC, 46/47, 49L, 104; Tanks Art Centre 7M; Tjapukai Aboriginal Cultural Park 8MR, 12; Tourism Port Douglas & Daintree 24/25, 82/83, 100MR; Tourism Queensland 99; Tourism Queensland 4MC, 8ML, 16, 48, 48/49, 56/57, 57L, 67L, 68, 69, 98; Treasury Casino and Hotel 109L; Village in the Rainforest 81L; Warner Village Theme Parks 4ML, 6ML, 8MC, 26, 27, 100MC

Cover credits: Richard Taylor/4Corners Images (main) Peter Stuckings/Apa Publications (bottom)

Printed by CTPS – China

DISTRIBUTION

UK, Ireland and Europe
Apa Publications (UK) Ltd
sales@insightguides.com
United States and Canada
Ingram Publisher Services
ips@ingramcontent.com
Australia and New Zealand
Woodslane
info@woodslane.com.au
Southeast Asia
Apa Publications (Singapore) Pte
singaporeoffice@insightguides.com
Worldwide
Apa Publications (UK) Ltd
sales@insightguides.com

INDEX

MAP LEGEND

★ Place of interest
ℹ Tourist information
𝐢 Statue/monument
✉ Main post office
🚌 Main bus station
☀ Viewpoint

☐ Park
▨ Important building
▨ Hotel
▨ Transport hub
▨ Market/store
☐ Pedestrian area
☐ Urban area

● Start of tour
→ Tour & route direction
❶ Recommended sight
❷ Recommended restaurant/café

INSIGHT ⊙ GUIDES
OFF THE SHELF

Since 1970, INSIGHT GUIDES has provided a unique perspective on the world's best travel destinations by using specially commissioned photography and illuminating text written by local authors.

Whether you're planning a city break, a walking tour or the journey of a lifetime, our superb range of guidebooks and phrasebooks will inspire you to discover more about your chosen destination.

INSIGHT GUIDES

offer a unique combination of stunning photos, absorbing narrative and detailed maps, providing all the inspiration and information you need.

PHRASEBOOKS & DICTIONARIES

help users to feel at home, when away. Pocket-sized with a free app to download, they go where you do.

CITY GUIDES

pack hundreds of great photos into a smaller format with detailed practical information, so you can navigate the world's top cities with confidence.

EXPLORE GUIDES

feature easy-to-follow walks and itineraries in the world's most exciting destinations, with our choice of the best places to eat and drink along the way.

POCKET GUIDES

combine concise information on where to go and what to do in a handy compact format, ideal on the ground. Includes a full-colour, fold-out map.

EXPERIENCE GUIDES

feature offbeat perspectives and secret gems for experienced travellers, with a collection of over 100 ideas for a memorable stay in a city.

www.insightguides.com